PENGUIN BOOKS

Innocence

Roald Dahl is best known for his mischievous, wildly inventive stories for children. But throughout his life he was also a prolific and acclaimed writer of stories for adults. These sinister, surprising tales continue to entertain, amuse and shock generations of readers even today.

PENGUIN BOOKS

UK | USA | Canada | Ireland | Australia
India | New Zealand | South Africa

Penguin Books is part of the Penguin Random House group of companies
whose addresses can be found at global.penguinrandomhouse.com.

These stories have been previously published in a variety of publications.
Details of each story's original publication are provided at the start of each
chapter and constitute an extension of this copyright page.
This collection first published in Penguin Books 2017

001

Set in 12.5/14.75 pt Garamond MT Std
Typeset by Palimpsest Book Production Limited, Falkirk, Stirlingshire
Printed in Great Britain by Clays Ltd, St Ives plc

A CIP catalogue record for this book is available from the British Library

ISBN: 978-1-405-93325-4

www.greenpenguin.co.uk

Contents

Boy

First published by *Jonathan Cape Ltd* (1984)

For Alfhild, Else, Asta, Ellen and Louis

An autobiography is a book a person writes about his own life and it is usually full of all sorts of boring details.

This is not an autobiography. I would never write a history of myself. On the other hand, throughout my young days at school and just afterwards a number of things happened to me that I have never forgotten.

None of these things is important, but each of them made such a tremendous impression on me that I have never been able to get them out of my mind. Each of them, even after a lapse of fifty and sometimes sixty years, has remained seared on my memory.

I didn't have to search for any of them. All I had to do was skim them off the top of my consciousness and write them down.

Some are funny. Some are painful. Some are unpleasant. I suppose that is why I have always remembered them so vividly. All are true.

R.D.

Wendy House

Alfhild Ellen and Else me and Astri
Radyr

Papa and Mama

My father, Harald Dahl, was a Norwegian who came from a small town near Oslo, called Sarpsborg. His own father, my grandfather, was a fairly prosperous merchant who owned a store in Sarpsborg and traded in just about everything from cheese to chicken-wire.

I am writing these words in 1984, but this grandfather of mine was born, believe it or not, in 1820, shortly after Wellington had defeated Napoleon at Waterloo. If my grandfather had been alive today he would have been one hundred and sixty-four years old. My father would have been one hundred and twenty-one. Both my father and my grandfather were late starters so far as children were concerned.

When my father was fourteen, which is still more than one hundred years ago, he was up on the roof of the family house replacing some loose tiles when he slipped and fell. He broke his left arm below the elbow. Somebody ran to fetch the doctor, and half an hour later this gentleman made a majestic and drunken arrival in his horse-drawn buggy. He was so drunk that he mistook the fractured elbow for a dislocated shoulder.

'We'll soon put this back into place!' he cried out, and two men were called off the street to help with the pulling. They were instructed to hold my father by the waist while the doctor grabbed him by the wrist of the broken arm and shouted, 'Pull men, pull! Pull as hard as you can!'

The pain must have been excruciating. The victim screamed, and his mother, who was watching the performance in horror, shouted 'Stop!' But by then the pullers had done so much damage that a splinter of bone was sticking out through the skin of the forearm.

This was in 1877 and orthopaedic surgery was not what it is today. So they simply amputated the arm at the elbow, and for the rest of his life my father had to manage with one arm. Fortunately, it was the left arm that he lost and gradually, over the years, he taught himself to do more or less anything he wanted with just the four fingers and thumb of his right hand. He could tie a shoelace as quickly as you or me, and for cutting up the food on his plate, he sharpened the bottom edge of a fork so that it served as both knife and fork all in one. He kept his ingenious instrument in a slim leather case and carried it in his pocket wherever he went. The loss of an arm, he used to say, caused him only one serious inconvenience. He found it impossible to cut the top off a boiled egg.

My father was a year or so older than his brother Oscar, but they were exceptionally close, and soon after they left school, they went for a long walk together to plan their future. They decided that a small town like Sarpsborg in a small country like Norway was no place in which to make a fortune. So what they must do, they agreed, was go away to one of the big countries, either to England or France, where opportunities to make good would be boundless.

Their own father, an amiable giant nearly seven foot tall, lacked the drive and ambition of his sons, and he refused to support this tomfool idea. When he forbade them to go, they ran away from home, and somehow or other the two of them managed to work their way to France on a cargo ship.

From Calais they went to Paris, and in Paris they agreed to separate because each of them wished to be independent of the other. Uncle Oscar, for some reason, headed west for La Rochelle on the Atlantic coast, while my father remained in Paris for the time being.

The story of how these two brothers each started a totally separate business in different countries and how each of them made a fortune is interesting, but there is no time to tell it here except in the briefest manner.

Take my Uncle Oscar first. La Rochelle was then, and still is, a fishing port. By the time he was forty he had become the wealthiest man in town. He owned a fleet of trawlers called 'Pêcheurs d'Atlantique' and a large canning factory to can the sardines his trawlers brought in. He acquired a wife from a good family and a magnificent town house as well as a large château in the country. He became a collector of Louis XV furniture, good pictures and rare books, and all these beautiful things together with the two properties are still in the family. I have not seen the château in the country, but I was in the La Rochelle house a couple of years ago and it really is something. The furniture alone should be in a museum.

While Uncle Oscar was bustling around in La Rochelle, his one-armed brother Harald (my own father) was not sitting on his rump doing nothing. He had met in Paris another young Norwegian called Aadnesen and the two of them now decided to form a partnership and become shipbrokers. A shipbroker is a person who supplies a ship with everything it needs when it comes into port – fuel and food, ropes and paint, soap and towels, hammers and nails, and thousands of other tiddly little items. A shipbroker is a kind of enormous shopkeeper for ships, and by far the most important item he supplies to them is the fuel on which the ship's engines run. In those days fuel meant only one thing. It meant coal. There were no oil-

burning motorships on the high seas at that time. All ships were steamships and these old steamers would take on hundreds and often thousands of tons of coal in one go. To the shipbrokers, coal was black gold.

My father and his new-found friend, Mr Aadnesen, understood all this very well. It made sense they told each other, to set up their shipbroking business in one of the great coaling ports of Europe. Which was it to be? The answer was simple. The greatest coaling port in the world at that time was Cardiff, in South Wales. So off to Cardiff they went, these two ambitious young men, carrying with them little or no luggage. But my father had something more delightful than luggage. He had a wife, a young French girl called Marie whom he had recently married in Paris.

In Cardiff, the shipbroking firm of 'Aadnesen & Dahl' was set up and a single room in Bute Street was rented as an office. From then on, we have what sounds like one of those exaggerated fairy-stories of success, but in reality it was the result of tremendous hard and brainy work by those two friends. Very soon 'Aadnesen & Dahl' had more business than the partners could handle alone. Larger office space was acquired and more staff were engaged. The real money then began rolling in. Within a few years, my father was able to buy a fine house in the village of Llandaff, just outside Cardiff, and there his wife Marie bore him two children, a girl and a boy. But tragically, she died after giving birth to the second child.

When the shock and sorrow of her death had begun to subside a little, my father suddenly realized that his two small children ought at the very least to have a stepmother to care for them. What is more, he felt terribly lonely. It was quite obvious that he must try to find himself another wife. But this was easier said than done for a Norwegian living in South Wales who didn't know very many people. So he decided to take a holiday and travel back to his own country, Norway, and who knows, he might if he was lucky find himself a lovely new bride in his own country.

Over in Norway, during the summer of 1911, while taking a trip in a small coastal steamer in the Oslofjord, he met a young lady called Sofie Magdalene Hesselberg. Being a fellow who knew a good thing when he saw one, he proposed to her within a week and married her soon after that.

Mama Engaged

Harald Dahl took his Norwegian wife on a honeymoon in Paris, and after that back to the house in Llandaff. The two of them were deeply in love and blissfully happy, and during the next six years she bore him four children, a girl,

me at 8 months

another girl, a boy (me) and a third girl. There were now six children in the family, two by my father's first wife and four by his second. A larger and grander house was needed and the money was there to buy it.

So in 1918, when I was two, we all moved into an imposing country mansion beside the village of Radyr, about eight miles west of Cardiff. I remember it as a mighty house with turrets on its roof and with majestic lawns and terraces all around it. There were many acres of farm and woodland, and a number of cottages for the staff. Very soon, the meadows were full of milking cows and the sties were full of pigs and the chicken-run was full of chickens. There were several massive shire-horses for pulling the ploughs and the hay-wagons, and there was a ploughman and a cowman and a couple of gardeners and

the house at Radyr

all manner of servants in the house itself. Like his brother Oscar in La Rochelle, Harald Dahl had made it in no uncertain manner.

But what interests me most of all about these two brothers, Harald and Oscar, is this. Although they came from a simple unsophisticated small-town family, both of them, quite independently of one another, developed a powerful interest in beautiful things. As soon as they could afford it, they began to fill their houses with lovely paintings and fine furniture. In addition to that, my father became an expert gardener and above all a collector of alpine plants. My mother used to tell me how the two of them would go on expeditions up into the mountains of Norway and how he would frighten her to death by climbing one-handed up steep cliff-faces to reach small alpine plants growing high up on some rocky ledge. He was also an accomplished wood-carver, and most of the mirror-frames in the house were his own work. So indeed was the entire mantelpiece around the fireplace in the living-room, a splendid design of fruit and foliage and intertwining branches carved in oak.

He was a tremendous diary-writer. I still have one of his many notebooks from the Great War of 1914–18. Every single day during those five war years he would write several pages of comment and observation about the events of the time. He wrote with a pen and although Norwegian was his mother-tongue, he always wrote his diaries in perfect English.

a letter from Papa

He harboured a curious theory about how to develop a sense of beauty in the minds of his children. Every time my mother became pregnant, he would wait until the last three months of her pregnancy and then he would announce to her that 'the glorious walks' must begin. These glorious walks consisted of him taking her to places of great beauty in the countryside and walking with her for about an hour each day so that she could absorb the splendour of the surroundings. His theory was that if the eye of a pregnant woman was constantly observing the beauty of nature, this beauty would somehow become transmitted to the mind of the unborn baby within her womb and that baby would grow up to be a lover of beautiful things. This was the treatment that all of his children received before they were born.

Kindergarten, 1922–3 (age 6–7)

In 1920, when I was still only three, my mother's eldest child, my own sister Astri, died from appendicitis. She was seven years old when she died, which was also the age of my own eldest daughter, Olivia, when she died from measles forty-two years later.

Astri was far and away my father's favourite. He adored her beyond measure and her sudden death left him literally speechless for days afterwards. He was so overwhelmed with grief that when he himself went down with pneumonia a month or so afterwards, he did not much care whether he lived or died.

If they had had penicillin in those days, neither appendicitis nor pneumonia would have been so much of a threat, but with no penicillin or any other magical antibiotic cures, pneumonia in particular was a very dangerous illness indeed. The pneumonia patient, on about the fourth or fifth day, would invariably reach what was known as 'the crisis'. The temperature soared and the pulse became rapid. The patient had to fight to survive. My father refused to fight. He was thinking, I am quite sure, of his beloved daughter, and he was wanting to join her in heaven. So he died. He was fifty-seven years old.

My mother had now lost a daughter and a husband all in the space of a few weeks. Heaven knows what it must have felt like to be hit with a double catastrophe like this. Here she was, a young Norwegian in a foreign land, suddenly having to face all alone the very gravest problems and responsibilities. She had five children to look after, three of her own and two by her husband's first wife, and to make matters worse, she herself was expecting another baby in two months' time. A less courageous woman would almost certainly have sold the house and packed her bags and headed straight back to Norway with the children. Over there in her own country she had her mother and father willing and waiting to help her, as well as her two unmarried sisters. But she refused to take the easy way out. Her husband had always stated most emphatically that he wished all his children to be educated

Me and Mama Radyrr

in English schools. They were the best in the world, he used to say. Better by far than the Norwegian ones. Better even than the Welsh ones, despite the fact that he lived in Wales and had his business there. He maintained that there was some kind of magic about English schooling and that the education it provided had caused the inhabitants of a small island to become a great nation and a great Empire and to produce the world's greatest literature. 'No child of mine', he kept saying, 'is going to school anywhere else but in England.' My mother was determined to carry out the wishes of her dead husband.

To accomplish this, she would have to move house from Wales to England, but she wasn't ready for that yet. She must stay here in Wales for a while longer, where she knew people who could help and advise her, especially her husband's great friend and partner, Mr Aadnesen. But even if she wasn't leaving Wales quite yet, it was essential that she move to a smaller and more manageable house. She had enough children to look after without having to bother about a farm as well. So as soon as her fifth child (another daughter) was born, she sold the big house and moved to a smaller one a few miles away in Llandaff. It was called Cumberland Lodge and it was nothing more than a pleasant medium-sized suburban villa. So it was in Llandaff two years later, when I was six years old, that I went to my first school.

The school was a kindergarten run by two sisters, Mrs Corfield and Miss Tucker, and it was called Elmtree House. It is astonishing how little one remembers about one's life before the age of seven or eight. I can tell you all

Me, six

sorts of things that happened to me from eight onwards, but only very few before that. I went for a whole year to Elmtree House but I cannot even remember what my classroom looked like. Nor can I picture the faces of Mrs Corfield or Miss Tucker, although I am sure they were sweet and smiling. I do have a blurred memory of sitting on the stairs and trying over and over again to tie one of my shoelaces, but that is all that comes back to me at this distance of the school itself.

On the other hand, I can remember very clearly the journeys I made to and from the school because they were so tremendously exciting. Great excitement is probably the only thing that really interests a six-year-old boy and it sticks in his mind. In my case, the excitement centred around my new tricycle. I rode to school on it every day with my eldest sister riding on hers. No grown-ups came with us, and I can remember oh so vividly how the two of us used to go racing at enormous tricycle speeds down the middle of the road and then, most glorious of all, when we came to a corner, we would lean to one side and take it on two wheels. All this, you must realize, was in the good old days when the sight of a motor-car on the street was an event, and it was quite safe for tiny children to go tricycling and whooping their way to school in the centre of the highway.

So much, then, for my memories of kindergarten sixty-two years ago. It's not much, but it's all there is left.

Llandaff Cathedral School,
1923–5
(age 7–9)

Else, me, Alfhild

A picnic with Mama

The bicycle and the sweet-shop

When I was seven, my mother decided I should leave kindergarten and go to a proper boy's school. By good fortune, there existed a well-known Preparatory School for boys about a mile from our house. It was called Llandaff Cathedral School, and it stood right under the shadow of Llandaff cathedral. Like the cathedral, the school is still there and still flourishing.

Llandaff Cathedral

But here again, I can remember very little about the two years I attended Llandaff Cathedral School, between the age of seven and nine. Only two moments remain clearly in my mind. The first lasted not more than five seconds but I will never forget it.

It was my first term and I was walking home alone across the village green after school when suddenly one of the senior twelve-year-old boys came riding full speed down the road on his bicycle about twenty yards away from me. The road was on a hill and the boy was going down the slope, and as he flashed by he started backpedalling very quickly so that the free-wheeling mechanism of his bike made a loud whirring sound. At the same time, he took his hands off the handlebars and folded them casually across his chest. I stopped dead and stared after him. How wonderful he was! How swift and brave and graceful in his long trousers with bicycle-clips around them and his scarlet school cap at a jaunty angle on his head! One day, I told myself, one glorious day I will have a bike like that and I will wear long trousers with bicycle-clips and my school cap will sit jaunty on my head and I will go whizzing down the hill pedalling backwards with no hands on the handlebars!

I promise you that if somebody had caught me by the shoulder at that moment and said to me, 'What is your greatest wish in life, little boy? What is your absolute ambition? To be a doctor? A fine musician? A painter? A writer? Or the Lord Chancellor?' I would have answered without hesitation that my only ambition, my hope, my longing was to have a bike like that and to go whizzing down the hill with no hands on the handlebars. It would be fabulous. It made me tremble just to think about it.

My second and only other memory of Llandaff Cathedral School is extremely bizarre. It happened a little over a year later, when I was just nine. By then I had made some friends and when I walked to school in the mornings I would start out alone but would pick up four other boys of my own age along the way. After school was over, the same four boys and I would set out together across the village green and through the village itself, heading for home. On the way to school and on the way back we always passed the sweet-shop. No we didn't, we never passed it. We always stopped. We lingered outside its rather small window gazing in at the big glass jars full of Bull's-eyes and Old Fashioned Humbugs and Strawberry Bonbons and Glacier Mints and Acid Drops and Pear Drops and Lemon Drops and all the rest of them. Each of us received sixpence a week for pocket-money, and whenever there was any money in our pockets, we would all troop in together to buy a pennyworth of this or that. My own favourites were Sherbet Suckers and Liquorice Bootlaces.

One of the other boys, whose name was Thwaites, told me I should never eat Liquorice Bootlaces. Thwaites's father, who was a doctor, had said that they were made from rats' blood. The father had given his young son a lecture about Liquorice Bootlaces when he had caught him eating one in bed. 'Every ratcatcher in the country', the father had said, 'takes his rats to the Liquorice Bootlace Factory, and the manager pays tuppence for each rat. Many a ratcatcher has become a millionaire by selling his dead rats to the Factory.'

'But how do they turn the rats into liquorice?' the young Thwaites had asked his father.

'They wait until they've got ten thousand rats,' the father had answered, 'then they dump them all into a huge shiny steel cauldron and boil them up for several hours. Two men stir the bubbling cauldron with long poles and in the end they have a thick steaming rat-stew. After that, a cruncher is lowered into the cauldron to crunch the bones, and what's left is a pulpy substance called rat-mash.'

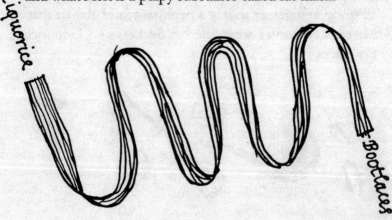

'Yes, but how do they turn that into Liquorice Boot-laces, Daddy?' the young Thwaites had asked, and this question, according to Thwaites, had caused his father to pause and think for a few moments before he answered it. At last he had said, 'The two men who were doing the stirring with the long poles now put on their wellington boots and climb into the cauldron and shovel the hot rat-mash out on to a concrete floor. Then they run a steam-roller over it several times to flatten it out. What is left looks rather like a gigantic black pancake, and all they have to do after that is to wait for it to cool and to harden so they can cut it up into strips to make the Bootlaces. Don't ever eat them,' the father had said. 'If you do, you'll get ratitis.'

'What is ratitis, Daddy?' young Thwaites had asked.

'All the rats that the rat-catchers catch are poisoned with rat-poison,' the father had said. 'It's the rat-poison that gives you ratitis.'

'Yes, but what happens to you when you catch it?' young Thwaites had asked.

'Your teeth become very sharp and pointed,' the father had answered. 'And a short stumpy tail grows out of your back just above your bottom. There is no cure for ratitis. I ought to know. I'm a doctor.'

We all enjoyed Thwaites's story and we made him tell it to us many times on our walks to and from school. But it didn't stop any of us except Thwaites from buying Liquorice Bootlaces. At two for a penny they were the best value in the shop. A Bootlace, in case you haven't had the pleasure of handling one, is not round. It's like a flat black tape about half an inch wide. You buy it rolled up in a coil, and in those days it used to be so long that when you unrolled it and held one end at arm's length above your head, the other end touched the ground.

Sherbet Suckers were also two a penny. Each Sucker consisted of a yellow cardboard tube filled with sherbet powder, and there was a hollow liquorice straw sticking out of it. (Rat's blood again, young Thwaites would warn us, pointing at the liquorice straw.) You sucked the sherbet up through the straw and when it was finished you ate the liquorice. They were delicious, those Sherbet Suckers. The sherbet fizzed in your mouth, and if you knew how to do it, you could make white froth come out of your nostrils and pretend you were throwing a fit.

Gobstoppers, costing a penny each, were enormous hard round balls the size of small tomatoes. One Gobstopper would provide about an hour's worth of non-stop sucking and if you took it out of your mouth and inspected it every five minutes or so, you would find it had changed colour. There was something fascinating about the way it went from pink to blue to green to yellow. We used to wonder how in the world the Gobstopper Factory managed to achieve this magic. 'How *does* it happen?' we would ask each other. 'How *can* they make it keep changing colour?'

'It's your spit that does it,' young Thwaites proclaimed. As the son of a doctor, he considered himself to be an authority on all things that had to do with the body. He could tell us about scabs and when they were ready to be picked off. He knew why a black eye was blue and why blood was red. 'It's your spit that makes a Gobstopper change colour,' he kept insisting. When we asked him to elaborate on this theory, he answered, 'You wouldn't understand it if I did tell you.'

Pear Drops were exciting because they had a dangerous taste. They smelled of nail-varnish and they froze the back of your throat. All of us were warned against eating them, and the result was that we ate them more than ever.

Then there was a hard brown lozenge called the Tonsil Tickler. The Tonsil Tickler tasted and smelled very strongly of chloroform. We had not the slightest doubt that these things were saturated in the dreaded anaesthetic which, as Thwaites had many times pointed out to us, could put you to sleep for hours at a stretch. 'If my father has to saw off somebody's leg,' he said, 'he pours chloroform on to a pad and the person sniffs it and goes to sleep and my father saws his leg off without him even feeling it.'

'But why do they put it into sweets and sell them to us?' we asked him.

You might think a question like this would have baffled Thwaites. But Thwaites was never baffled. 'My father says Tonsil Ticklers were invented for dangerous prisoners in jail,' he said. 'They give them one with each meal and the chloroform makes them sleepy and stops them rioting.'

'Yes,' we said, 'but why sell them to children?'

'It's a plot,' Thwaites said. 'A grown-up plot to keep us quiet.'

The sweet-shop in Llandaff in the year 1923 was the very centre of our lives. To us, it was what a bar is to a drunk, or a church is to a Bishop. Without it, there would have been little to live for. But it had one terrible drawback, this sweet-shop. The woman who owned it was a horror. We hated her and we had good reason for doing so.

Her name was Mrs Pratchett. She was a small skinny old hag with a moustache on her upper lip and a mouth as sour as a green gooseberry. She never smiled. She never welcomed us when we went in, and the only times she spoke were when she said things like, 'I'm watchin' you so keep yer thievin' fingers off them chocolates!' Or 'I don't want you in 'ere just to look around! Either you *forks* out or you *gets* out!'

But by far the most loathsome thing about Mrs Pratchett was the filth that clung around her. Her apron was grey and greasy. Her blouse had bits of breakfast all over it, toast-crumbs and tea stains and splotches of dried egg-yolk. It was her hands, however, that disturbed us most. They were disgusting. They were black with dirt and grime. They looked as though they had been putting lumps of coal on the fire all day long. And do not forget please that it was these very hands and fingers that she plunged into the sweet-jars when we asked for a penny-worth of Treacle Toffee or Wine Gums or Nut Clusters or whatever. There were precious few health laws in those days, and nobody, least of all Mrs Pratchett, ever thought of using a little shovel for getting out the sweets as they do today. The mere sight of her grimy right hand with its black fingernails digging an ounce of Chocolate Fudge out of a jar would have caused a starving tramp to go running from the shop. But not us. Sweets were our life-blood. We would have put up with far worse than that to get them. So we simply stood and watched in sullen silence while this disgusting old woman stirred around inside the jars with her foul fingers.

The other thing we hated Mrs Pratchett for was her meanness. Unless you spent a whole sixpence all in one go, she wouldn't give you a bag. Instead you got your sweets twisted up in a small piece of newspaper which she tore off a pile of old *Daily Mirrors* lying on the counter.

So you can well understand that we had it in for Mrs Pratchett in a big way, but we didn't quite know what to do about it. Many schemes were put forward but none of them was any good. None of them, that is, until suddenly, one memorable afternoon, we found the dead mouse.

The Great Mouse Plot

My four friends and I had come across a loose floor-board at the back of the classroom, and when we prised it up with the blade of a pocket-knife, we discovered a big hollow space underneath. This, we decided, would be our secret hiding place for sweets and other small treasures such as conkers and monkey-nuts and birds' eggs. Every afternoon, when the last lesson was over, the five of us would wait until the classroom had emptied, then we would lift up the floor-board and examine our secret hoard, perhaps adding to it or taking something away.

One day, when we lifted it up, we found a dead mouse lying among our treasures. It was an exciting discovery. Thwaites took it out by its tail and waved it in front of our faces. 'What shall we do with it?' he cried.

'It stinks!' someone shouted. 'Throw it out of the window quick!'

'Hold on a tick,' I said. 'Don't throw it away.'

Thwaites hesitated. They all looked at me.

When writing about oneself, one must strive to be truthful. Truth is more important than modesty. I must tell you, therefore, that it was I and I alone who had the idea for the great and daring Mouse Plot. We all have our moments of brilliance and glory, and this was mine.

'Why don't we', I said, 'slip it into one of Mrs Pratchett's jars of sweets? Then when she puts her dirty hand in to grab a handful, she'll grab a stinky dead mouse instead.'

The other four stared at me in wonder. Then, as the sheer genius of the plot began to sink in, they all started grinning. They slapped me on the back. They cheered me and danced around the classroom. 'We'll do it today!' they cried. 'We'll do it on the way home! *You* had the idea,' they said to me, 'so *you* can be the one to put the mouse in the jar.'

Thwaites handed me the mouse. I put it into my trouser pocket. Then the five of us left the school, crossed the village green and headed for the sweet-shop. We were tremendously jazzed up. We felt like a gang of desperados setting out to rob a train or blow up the sheriff's office.

'Make sure you put it into a jar which is used often,' somebody said.

'I'm putting it in Gobstoppers,' I said. 'The Gobstopper jar is never behind the counter.'

'I've got a penny,' Thwaites said, 'so I'll ask for one Sherbet Sucker and one Bootlace. And while she turns away to get them, you slip the mouse in quickly with the Gobstoppers.'

Thus everything was arranged. We were strutting a little as we entered the shop. We were the victors now and Mrs Pratchett was the victim. She stood behind the counter, and her small malignant pig-eyes watched us suspiciously as we came forward.'

'One Sherbet Sucker, please,' Thwaites said to her, holding out his penny.

I kept to the rear of the group, and when I saw Mrs Pratchett turn her head away for a couple of seconds to fish a Sherbet Sucker out of the box, I lifted the heavy glass lid of the Gobstopper jar and dropped the mouse in. Then I replaced the lid as silently as possible. My heart was thumping like mad and my hands had gone all sweaty.

'And one Bootlace, please,' I heard Thwaites saying. When I turned round, I saw Mrs Pratchett holding out the Bootlace in her filthy fingers.

'I don't want all the lot of you troopin' in 'ere if only one of you is buyin',' she screamed at us. 'Now beat it! Go on, get out!'

As soon as we were outside, we broke into a run. 'Did you do it?' they shouted at me.

'Of course I did!' I said.

'Well done you!' they cried. 'What a super show!'

I felt like a hero. I *was* a hero. It was marvellous to be so popular.

Mr Coombes

The flush of triumph over the dead mouse was carried forward to the next morning as we all met again to walk to school.

'Let's go in and see if it's still in the jar,' somebody said as we approached the sweet-shop.

'Don't,' Thwaites said firmly. 'It's too dangerous. Walk past as though nothing has happened.'

As we came level with the shop we saw a cardboard notice hanging on the door.

We stopped and stared. We had never known the sweet-shop to be closed at this time in the morning, even on Sundays.

'What's happened?' we asked each other. 'What's going on?'

We pressed our faces against the window and looked inside. Mrs Pratchett was nowhere to be seen.

'Look!' I cried. 'The Gobstopper jar's gone! It's not on the shelf! There's a gap where it used to be!'

'It's on the floor!' someone said. 'It's smashed to bits and there's Gobstoppers everywhere!'

'There's the mouse!' someone else shouted.

We could see it all, the huge glass jar smashed to smithereens with the dead mouse lying in the wreckage and hundreds of many-coloured Gobstoppers littering the floor.

'She got such a shock when she grabbed hold of the mouse that she dropped everything,' somebody was saying.

'But why didn't she sweep it all up and open the shop?' I asked.

Nobody answered me.

We turned away and walked towards the school. All of a sudden we had begun to feel slightly uncomfortable. There was something not quite right about the shop being closed. Even Thwaites was unable to offer a reasonable explanation. We became silent. There was a faint scent of danger in the air now. Each one of us had caught a whiff of it. Alarm bells were beginning to ring faintly in our ears.

After a while, Thwaites broke the silence. 'She must have got one heck of a shock,' he said. He paused. We all looked at him, wondering what wisdom the great medical authority was going to come out with next.

'After all,' he went on, 'to catch hold of a dead mouse when you're expecting to catch hold of a Gobstopper must be a pretty frightening experience. Don't you agree?'

Nobody answered him.

'Well now,' Thwaites went on, 'when an old person like

Mrs Pratchett suddenly gets a very big shock, I suppose you know what happens next?'

'What?' we said. 'What happens?'

'You ask my father,' Thwaites said. 'He'll tell you.'

'You tell us,' we said.

'It gives her a heart attack,' Thwaites announced. 'Her heart stops beating and she's dead in five seconds.'

For a moment or two my own heart stopped beating. Thwaites pointed a finger at me and said darkly, 'I'm afraid you've killed her.'

'*Me*?' I cried. 'Why just *me*?'

'It was *your* idea,' he said. 'And what's more, *you* put the mouse in.'

All of a sudden, I was a murderer.

At exactly that point, we heard the school bell ringing in the distance and we had to gallop the rest of the way so as not to be late for prayers.

Prayers were held in the Assembly Hall. We all perched in rows on wooden benches while the teachers sat up on the platform in armchairs, facing us. The five of us scrambled into our places just as the Headmaster marched in, followed by the rest of the staff.

The Headmaster is the only teacher at Llandaff Cathedral School that I can remember, and for a reason you will soon discover, I can remember him very clearly indeed. His name was Mr Coombes and I have a picture in my mind of a giant of a man with a face like a ham and a mass of rusty-coloured hair that sprouted in a tangle all over the top of his head. All grown-ups appear as giants to small children. But Headmasters (and policemen) are the biggest giants of all and acquire a marvellously exaggerated stature. It is possible that Mr Coombes was a perfectly normal being, but in my memory he was a giant, a tweed-suited giant who always wore a black gown over his tweeds and a waistcoat under his jacket.

Mr Coombes now proceeded to mumble through the same old prayers we had every day, but this morning, when the last amen had been spoken, he did not turn and lead his group rapidly out of the Hall as usual. He remained standing before us, and it was clear he had an announcement to make.

'The whole school is to go out and line up around the playground immediately,' he said. 'Leave your books behind. And no talking.'

Mr Coombes was looking grim. His hammy pink face had taken on that dangerous scowl which only appeared when he was extremely cross and somebody was for the high-jump. I sat there small and frightened among the rows and rows of other boys, and to me at that moment the Headmaster, with his black gown draped over his shoulders, was like a judge at a murder trial.

'He's after the killer,' Thwaites whispered to me.

I began to shiver.

'I'll bet the police are here already,' Thwaites went on. 'And the Black Maria's waiting outside.'

As we made our way out to the playground, my whole stomach began to feel as though it was slowly filling up with swirling water. *I am only eight years old*, I told myself. *No little boy of eight has ever murdered anyone. It's not possible*.

Out in the playground on this warm cloudy September morning, the Deputy Headmaster was shouting, 'Line up in forms! Sixth Form over there! Fifth Form next to them! Spread out! Spread out! Get on with it! Stop talking all of you!'

Thwaites and I and my other three friends were in the Second Form, the lowest but one, and we lined up against the red-brick wall of the playground shoulder to shoulder. I can remember that when every boy in the school was in his place, the line stretched right round the four sides of the playground – about one hundred small boys altogether, aged between six and twelve, all of us wearing identical grey shorts and grey blazers and grey stockings and black shoes.

'Stop that *talking*!' shouted the Deputy Head. 'I want absolute silence!'

But why for heaven's sake were we in the playground at all? I wondered. And why were we lined up like this? It had never happened before.

I half-expected to see two policemen come bounding out of the school to grab me by the arms and put handcuffs on my wrists.

A single door led out from the school on to the playground. Suddenly it swung open and through it, like the angel of death, strode Mr Coombes, huge and bulky in his tweed suit and black gown, and beside him, believe it or not, right beside him trotted the tiny figure of Mrs Pratchett herself!

Mrs Pratchett was alive!

The relief was tremendous.

'She's alive!' I whispered to Thwaites standing next to me. 'I didn't kill her!' Thwaites ignored me.

'We'll start over here,' Mr Coombes was saying to Mrs Pratchett. He grasped her by one of her skinny arms and led her over to where the Sixth Form was standing. Then, still keeping hold of her arm, he proceeded to lead her at a brisk walk down the line of boys. It was like someone inspecting the troops.

'What on earth are they doing?' I whispered.

Thwaites didn't answer me. I glanced at him. He had gone rather pale.

'Too big,' I heard Mrs Pratchett saying. 'Much too big. It's none of this lot. Let's 'ave a look at some of them titchy ones.'

Mr Coombes increased his pace. 'We'd better go all the way round,' he said. He seemed in a hurry to get it over with now and I could see Mrs Pratchett's skinny goat's legs trotting to keep up with him. They had already inspected one side of the playground where the Sixth Form and half the Fifth Form were standing. We watched them moving down the second side . . . then the third side.

'Still too big,' I heard Mrs Pratchett croaking. 'Much too big! Smaller than these! Much smaller! Where's them nasty little ones?'

They were coming closer to us now . . . closer and closer.

They were starting on the fourth side . . .

Every boy in our form was watching Mr Coombes and Mrs Pratchett as they came walking down the line towards us.

'Nasty cheeky lot, these little 'uns!' I heard Mrs Pratchett muttering. 'They comes into my shop and they thinks they can do what they damn well likes!'

Mr Coombes made no reply to this.

'They nick things when I ain't looking',' she went on. 'They put their grubby 'ands all over everything and they've got no manners. I don't mind girls. I never 'ave no trouble with girls, but boys is 'ideous and 'orrible! I don't 'ave to tell *you* that, 'Eadmaster, do I?'

'These are the smaller ones,' Mr Coombes said.

I could see Mrs Pratchett's piggy little eyes staring hard at the face of each boy she passed.

Suddenly she let out a high-pitched yell and pointed a dirty finger straight at Thwaites. 'That's 'im!' she yelled. 'That's one of 'em! I'd know 'im a mile away, the scummy little bounder!'

The entire school turned to look at Thwaites. 'W-what have *I* done?' he stuttered, appealing to Mr Coombes.

'Shut up,' Mr Coombes said.

Mrs Pratchett's eyes flicked over and settled on my own face. I looked down and studied the black asphalt surface of the playground.

''Ere's another of 'em!' I heard her yelling. 'That one there!' She was pointing at me now.

'You're quite sure?' Mr Coombes said.

'Of course I'm sure!' she cried. 'I never forgets a face, least of all when it's as sly as that! 'Ee's one of 'em all right! There was five altogether! Now where's them other three?'

The other three, as I knew very well, were coming up next.

Mrs Pratchett's face was glimmering with venom as her eyes travelled beyond me down the line.

'There they are!' she cried out, stabbing the air with her finger. "*Im* . . . and *'im* . . . and *'im*! That's the five of 'em all right! We don't need to look no farther than this, 'Eadmaster! They're all 'ere, the nasty dirty little pigs! You've got their names, 'ave you?'

'I've got their names, Mrs Pratchett,' Mr Coombes told her. 'I'm much obliged to you.'

'And I'm much obliged to *you*, 'Eadmaster,' she answered.

As Mr Coombes led her away across the playground, we heard her saying, 'Right in the jar of Gobstoppers it was! A stinkin' dead mouse which I will never forget as long as I live!'

'You have my deepest sympathy,' Mr Coombes was muttering.

'Talk about shocks!' she went on. 'When my fingers caught 'old of that nasty soggy stinkin' dead mouse ...' Her voice trailed away as Mr Coombes led her quickly through the door into the school building.

Mrs Pratchett's revenge

Our form master came into the classroom with a piece of paper in his hand. 'The following are to report to the Headmaster's study at once,' he said. 'Thwaites . . . Dahl . . .' And then he read out the other three names which I have forgotten.

The five of us stood up and left the room. We didn't speak as we made our way down the long corridor into the Headmaster's private quarters where the dreaded study was situated. Thwaites knocked on the door.

'Enter!'

We sidled in. The room smelled of leather and tobacco. Mr Coombes was standing in the middle of it, dominating everything, a giant of a man if ever there was one, and in his hands he held a long yellow cane which curved round the top like a walking stick.

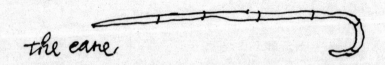

the cane

'I don't want any lies,' he said. 'I know very well you did it and you were all in it together. Line up over there against the bookcase.'

We lined up, Thwaites in front and I, for some reason, at the very back. I was last in the line.

'You,' Mr Coombes said, pointing the cane at Thwaites, 'Come over here.'

Thwaites went forward very slowly.

'Bend over,' Mr Coombes said.

Thwaites bent over. Our eyes were riveted on him. We were hypnotized by it all. We knew, of course, that boys got the cane now and again, but we had never heard of anyone being made to watch.

'Tighter, boy, tighter!' Mr Coombes snapped out. 'Touch the ground!'

Thwaites touched the carpet with the tips of his fingers.

Mr Coombes stood back and took up a firm stance with his legs well apart. I thought how small Thwaites's bottom looked and how very tight it was. Mr Coombes had his eyes focused squarely upon it. He raised the cane high above his shoulder, and as he brought it down, it made a loud swishing sound, and then there was a crack like a pistol shot as it struck Thwaites's bottom.

Little Thwaites seemed to lift about a foot into the air and he yelled 'Ow-w-w-w-w-w-w-w-w-w!' and straightened up like elastic.

'*Arder!*' shrieked a voice from over in the corner.

Now it was our turn to jump. We looked round and there, sitting in one of Mr Coombes's big leather armchairs, was the tiny loathsome figure of Mrs Pratchett! She was bounding up and down with excitement. 'Lay it into 'im!' she was shrieking. 'Let 'im 'ave it! Teach 'im a lesson!'

'Get down, boy!' Mr Coombes ordered. 'And stay down! You get an extra one every time you straighten up!'

'That's tellin' 'im!' shrieked Mrs Pratchett. 'That's tellin' the little blighter!'

I could hardly believe what I was seeing. It was like some awful pantomime. The violence was bad enough, and being made to watch it was even worse, but with Mrs Pratchett in the audience the whole thing became a nightmare.

Swish-crack! went the cane.

'Ow-w-w-w-w!' yelled Thwaites.

''Arder!' shrieked Mrs Pratchett. 'Stitch 'im up! Make it sting! Tickle 'im up good and proper! Warm 'is backside for 'im! Go on, warm it up, 'Eadmaster!'

Thwaites received four strokes, and by gum, they were four real whoppers.

'Next!' snapped Mr Coombes.

Thwaites came hopping past us on his toes, clutching his bottom with both hands and yelling, 'Ow! Ouch! Ouch! Ouch! Owwwww!'

With tremendous reluctance, the next boy sidled forward to his fate. I stood there wishing I hadn't been last in the line. The watching and waiting were probably even greater torture than the event itself.

Mr Coombes's performance the second time was the same as the first. So was Mrs Pratchett's. She kept up her screeching all the way through, exhorting Mr Coombes to greater and still greater efforts, and the awful thing was that he seemed to be responding to her cries. He was like an athlete who is spurred on by the shouts of the crowd

in the stands. Whether this was true or not, I was sure of one thing. He wasn't weakening.

My own turn came at last. My mind was swimming and my eyes had gone all blurry as I went forward to bend over. I can remember wishing my mother would suddenly come bursting into the room shouting, 'Stop! How dare you do that to my son!' But she didn't. All I heard was Mrs Pratchett's dreadful high-pitched voice behind me screeching, 'This one's the cheekiest of the bloomin' lot, 'Eadmaster! Make sure you let 'im 'ave it good and strong!'

Mr Coombes did just that. As the first stroke landed and the pistol-crack sounded, I was thrown forward so violently that if my fingers hadn't been touching the carpet, I think I would have fallen flat on my face. As it was, I was able to catch myself on the palms of my hands and keep my balance. At first I heard only the *crack* and felt absolutely nothing at all, but a fraction of a second later the burning sting that flooded across my buttocks was so terrific that all I could do was gasp. I gave a great gushing gasp that emptied my lungs of every breath of air that was in them.

It felt, I promise you, as though someone had laid a red-hot poker against my flesh and was pressing down on it hard.

The second stroke was worse than the first and this was probably because Mr Coombes was well practised and had a splendid aim. He was able, so it seemed, to land the second one almost exactly across the narrow line where the first one had struck. It is bad enough when the cane lands on fresh skin, but when it comes down on bruised and wounded flesh, the agony is unbelievable.

The third one seemed even worse than the second. Whether or not the wily Mr Coombes had chalked the cane beforehand and had thus made an aiming mark on my grey flannel shorts after the first stroke, I do not know. I am inclined to doubt it because he must have known that this was a practice much frowned upon by Headmasters in general in those days. It was not only regarded as unsporting, it was also an admission that you were not an expert at the job.

By the time the fourth stroke was delivered, my entire backside seemed to be going up in flames.

Far away in the distance, I heard Mr Coombes's voice saying, 'Now get out.'

As I limped across the study clutching my buttocks hard with both hands, a cackling sound came from the armchair over in the corner, and then I heard the vinegary voice of Mrs Pratchett saying, 'I am much obliged to you, 'Eadmaster, very much obliged. I don't think we is goin' to see any more stinkin' mice in my Gobstoppers from now on.'

When I returned to the classroom my eyes were wet with tears and everybody stared at me. My bottom hurt when I sat down at my desk.

That evening after supper my three sisters had their baths before me. Then it was my turn, but as I was about to step into the bathtub, I heard a horrified gasp from my mother behind me.

'What's this?' she gasped. 'What's happened to you?' She was staring at my bottom. I myself had not inspected it up to then, but when I twisted my head around and took a look at one of my buttocks, I saw the scarlet stripes and the deep blue bruising in between.

'Who did this?' my mother cried. 'Tell me at once!'

In the end I had to tell her the whole story, while my three sisters (aged nine, six and four) stood around in their nighties listening goggle-eyed. My mother heard me out in silence. She asked no questions. She just let me talk, and when I had finished, she said to our nurse, 'You get them into bed, Nanny. I'm going out.'

If I had had the slightest idea of what she was going to do next, I would have tried to stop her, but I hadn't. She went straight downstairs and put on her hat. Then she marched out of the house, down the drive and on to the road. I saw her through my bedroom window as she went out of the gates and turned left, and I remember calling out to her to come back, come back, come back. But she took no notice of me. She was walking very quickly, with her head held high and her body erect, and by the look of things I figured that Mr Coombes was in for a hard time.

About an hour later, my mother returned and came upstairs to kiss us all goodnight. 'I wish you hadn't done that,' I said to her. 'It makes me look silly.'

'They don't beat small children like that where I come from,' she said. 'I won't allow it.'

'What did Mr Coombes say to you, Mama?'

'He told me I was a foreigner and I didn't understand how British schools were run,' she said.

'Did he get ratty with you?'

'Very ratty,' she said. 'He told me that if I didn't like his methods I could take you away.'

'What did you say?'

'I said I would, as soon as the school year is finished. I shall find you an *English* school this time,' she said. 'Your father was right. English schools are the best in the world.'

'Does that mean it'll be a boarding school?' I asked.

'It'll have to be,' she said. 'I'm not quite ready to move the whole family to England yet.'

So I stayed on at Llandaff Cathedral School until the end of the summer term.

Going to Norway

The summer holidays! Those magic words! The mere mention of them used to send shivers of joy rippling over my skin.

All my summer holidays, from when I was four years old to when I was seventeen (1920 to 1932), were totally idyllic. This, I am certain, was because we always went to the same idyllic place and that place was Norway.

Except for my ancient half-sister and my not-quite-so-ancient half-brother, the rest of us were all pure Norwegian by blood. We all spoke Norwegian and all our relations

lived over there. So in a way, going to Norway every summer was like going home.

Even the journey was an event. Do not forget that there were no commercial aeroplanes in those times, so it took us four whole days to complete the trip out and another four days to get home again.

We were always an enormous party. There were my three sisters and my ancient half-sister (that's four), and my half-brother and me (that's six), and my mother (that's seven), and Nanny (that's eight), and in addition to these, there were never less than two others who were some sort of anonymous ancient friends of the ancient half-sister (that's ten altogether).

Looking back on it now, I don't know how my mother did it. There were all those train bookings and boat bookings and hotel bookings to be made in advance by letter. She had to make sure that we had enough shorts and shirts and sweaters and gymshoes and bathing costumes (you couldn't even buy a shoelace on the island we were going to), and the packing must have been a nightmare. Six huge trunks were carefully packed, as well as countless suitcases, and when the great departure day arrived, the ten of us, together with our mountains of luggage, would set out on the first and easiest step of the journey, the train to London.

When we arrived in London, we tumbled into three taxis and went clattering across the great city to King's Cross, where we got on to the train for Newcastle, two hundred miles to the north. The trip to Newcastle took about five hours, and when we arrived there, we needed three more taxis to take us from the station to the docks, where our boat would be waiting. The next stop after that would be Oslo, the capital of Norway.

When I was young, the capital of Norway was not called Oslo. It was called Christiania. But somewhere along the line, the Norwegians decided to do away with that pretty name and call it Oslo instead. As children, we always knew it as Christiania, but if I call it that here we shall only get confused, so I had better stick to Oslo all the way through.

The sea journey from Newcastle to Oslo took two days and a night, and if it was rough, as it often was, all of us got seasick except our dauntless mother. We used to lie in deck-chairs on the promenade deck, within easy reach of the rails, embalmed in rugs, our faces slate-grey and our stomachs churning, refusing the hot soup and ship's biscuits the kindly steward kept offering us. And as for poor Nanny, she began to feel sick the moment she set foot on deck. 'I hate these things!' she used to say. 'I'm sure we'll never get there! Which lifeboat do we go to when it starts to sink?' Then she would retire to her cabin, where she stayed groaning and trembling until the ship was firmly tied up at the quayside in Oslo harbour the next day.

We always stopped off for one night in Oslo so that we could have a grand annual family reunion with Bestemama and Bestepapa, our mother's parents, and with her two maiden sisters (our aunts) who lived in the same house.

When we got off the boat, we all went in a cavalcade of taxis straight to the Grand Hotel, where we would sleep one night, to drop off our luggage. Then, keeping the same taxis, we drove on to the grandparents' house, where an emotional welcome awaited us. All of us were embraced and kissed many times and tears flowed down wrinkled old cheeks and suddenly that quiet gloomy house came alive with many children's voices.

Ever since I first saw her, Bestemama was terrifically ancient. She was a white-haired wrinkly-faced old bird who seemed always to be sitting in her rocking-chair, rocking away and smiling benignly at this vast influx of grandchildren who barged in from miles away to take over her house for a few hours every year.

Bestepapa was the quiet one. He was a small dignified scholar with a white goatee beard, and as far as I could gather, he was an astrologer, a meteorologist and a speaker of ancient Greek. Like Bestemama, he sat most of the time quietly in a chair, saying very little and totally overwhelmed, I imagine, by the raucous rabble who were destroying his neat and polished home. The two things I remember most about Bestepapa were that he wore black boots and that he smoked an extraordinary pipe. The bowl of his pipe was made of meerschaum clay, and it had a flexible stem about three feet long so that the bowl rested on his lap.

All the grown-ups including Nanny, and all the children, even when the youngest was only a year old, sat down around the big oval dining-room table on the afternoon of our arrival, for the great annual celebration feast with the grandparents, and the food we received never varied. This was a Norwegian household, and for the Norwegians the best food in the world is fish. And when

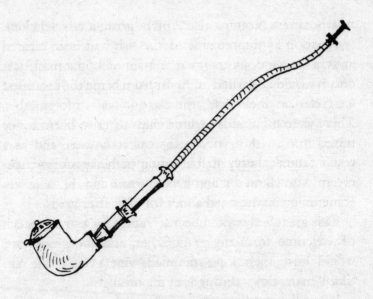

they say fish, they don't mean the sort of thing you and I get from the fishmonger. They mean *fresh fish*, fish that has been caught no more than twenty-four hours before and has never been frozen or chilled on a block of ice. I agree with them that the proper way to prepare fish like this is to poach it, and that is what they do with the finest specimens. And Norwegians, by the way, always eat the skin of the boiled fish, which they say has the best taste of all.

So naturally this great celebration feast started with fish. A massive fish, a flounder as big as a tea-tray and as thick as your arm was brought to the table. It had nearly black skin on top which was covered with brilliant orange spots, and it had, of course, been perfectly poached. Large white hunks of this fish were carved out and put on to our plates, and with it we had hollandaise sauce and boiled new potatoes. Nothing else. And by gosh, it was delicious.

As soon as the remains of the fish had been cleared away, a tremendous craggy mountain of home-made ice-cream would be carried in. Apart from being the creamiest ice-cream in the world, the flavour was unforgettable. There were thousands of little chips of crisp burnt toffee mixed into it (the Norwegians call it *krokan*), and as a result it didn't simply melt in your mouth like ordinary ice-cream. You chewed it and it went *crunch* and the taste was something you dreamed about for days afterwards.

This great feast would be interrupted by a small speech of welcome from my grandfather, and the grown-ups would raise their long-stemmed wine glasses and say 'skaal' many times throughout the meal.

When the guzzling was over, those who were considered old enough were given small glasses of home-made liqueur, a colourless but fiery drink that smelled of mulberries. The glasses were raised again and again, and the 'skaaling' seemed to go on for ever. In Norway, you may select any individual around the table and skaal him or her in a small private ceremony. You first lift your glass high and call out the name. 'Bestemama!' you say. 'Skaal, Bestemama!'

She will then lift her own glass and hold it up high. At the same time your own eyes meet hers, and you *must* keep looking deep into her eyes as you sip your drink. After you have both done this, you raise your glasses high up again in a sort of silent final salute, and only then does each person look away and set down his glass. It is a serious and solemn ceremony, and as a rule on formal occasions

Bestemama and Bestepapa (and Astri)

everyone skaals everyone else round the table once. If there are, for example, ten people present and you are one of them, you will skaal your nine companions once each individually, and you yourself will also receive nine separate skaals at different times during the meal – eighteen in all. That's how they work it in polite society over there, at least they used to in the old days, and quite a business it was. By the time I was ten, I would be permitted to take part in these ceremonies, and I always finished up as tipsy as a lord.

The magic island

The next morning, everyone got up early and eager to continue the journey. There was another full day's travelling to be done before we reached our final destination, most of it by boat. So after a rapid breakfast, our cavalcade left the Grand Hotel in three more taxis and headed for Oslo docks. There we went on board a small coastal steamer, and Nanny was heard to say, 'I'm sure it leaks! We shall all be food for the fishes before the day is out!' Then she would disappear below for the rest of the trip.

Fra Havna, Rössesund   Eneret A. Mathisen fotografi

We loved this part of the journey. The splendid little vessel with its single tall funnel would move out into the calm waters of the fjord and proceed at a leisurely pace along the coast, stopping every hour or so at a small wooden jetty where a group of villagers and summer people would be waiting to welcome friends or to collect parcels and mail. Unless you have sailed down the Oslofjord like this yourself on a tranquil summer's day, you cannot imagine what it is like. It is impossible to describe the sensation of absolute peace and beauty that surrounds you. The boat weaves in and out between countless tiny islands, some with small brightly painted wooden houses on them, but many with not a house or a tree on the bare rocks. These granite rocks are so smooth that you can lie and sun yourself on them in your bathing-costume without putting a towel underneath. We would see long-legged girls and tall boys basking on the rocks of the islands. There are no sandy beaches on the fjord. The rocks go straight down to the water's edge and the water is immediately deep. As a result, Norwegian children all learn to swim when they are very young because if you can't swim it is difficult to find a place to bathe.

Sometimes when our little vessel slipped between two small islands, the channel was so narrow we could almost touch the rocks on either side. We would pass row-boats and canoes with flaxen-haired children in them, their skins browned by the sun, and we would wave to them and watch their tiny boats rocking violently in the swell that our larger ship left behind.

Late in the afternoon, we would come finally to the end

of the journey, the island of Töme. This was where our mother always took us. Heaven knows how she found it, but to us it was the greatest place on earth. About two hundred yards from the jetty, along a narrow dusty road, stood a simple wooden hotel painted white. It was run by an elderly couple whose faces I still remember vividly, and every year they welcomed us like old friends. Everything about the hotel was extremely primitive, except the dining-room. The walls, the ceiling and the floor of our bedrooms were made of plain unvarnished pine planks. There was a washbasin and a jug of cold water in each of them. The lavatories were in a rickety wooden outhouse at the back of the hotel and each cubicle contained nothing more than a round hole cut in a piece of wood. You sat on the hole and what you did there dropped into a pit ten feet below. If you looked down the hole, you would often see rats scurrying about in the gloom. All this we took for granted.

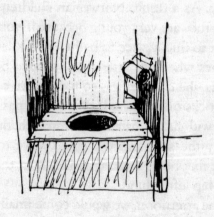

Breakfast was the best meal of the day in our hotel, and it was all laid out on a huge table in the middle of the dining-room from which you helped yourself. There were maybe fifty different dishes to choose from on that table. There were large jugs of milk, which all Norwegian children drink at every meal. There were plates of cold beef, veal, ham and pork. There was cold boiled mackerel submerged in aspic. There were spiced and pickled herring fillets, sardines, smoked eels and cod's roe. There was a large bowl piled high with hot boiled eggs. There were cold omelettes with chopped ham in them, and cold chicken and hot coffee for the grown-ups, and hot crisp rolls baked in the hotel kitchen, which we ate with butter and cranberry jam. There were stewed apricots and five or six different cheeses including of course the ever-present gjetost, that tall brown rather sweet Norwegian goat's cheese which you find on just about every table in the land.

After breakfast, we collected our bathing things and the whole party, all ten of us, would pile into our boat.

Everyone has some sort of a boat in Norway. Nobody sits around in front of the hotel. Nor does anyone sit on the beach because there aren't any beaches to sit on. In the early days, we had only a row-boat, but a very fine one it was. It carried all of us easily, with places for two rowers. My mother took one pair of oars and my fairly ancient half-brother took the other, and off we would go.

My mother and the half-brother (he was somewhere around eighteen then) were expert rowers. They kept in perfect time and the oars went *click-click, click-click* in their wooden rowlocks, and the rowers never paused once during the long forty-minute journey. The rest of us sat in the boat trailing our fingers in the clear water and looking for jelly-fish. We skimmed across the sound and went whizzing through narrow channels with rocky islands on either side, heading as always for a very secret tiny patch of sand on a distant island that only we knew about. In the early days we needed a place like this where we could paddle and play about because my youngest sister was only one, the next sister was three and I was four. The rocks and the deep water were no good to us.

Every day, for several summers, that tiny secret sand-patch on that tiny secret island was our regular destination. We would stay there for three or four hours, messing about in the water and in the rockpools and getting extraordinarily sunburnt.

Me, Alfhild, Else Norway 1924

In later years, when we were all a little older and could swim, the daily routine became different. By then, my mother had acquired a motor-boat, a small and not very seaworthy white wooden vessel which sat far too low in the water and was powered by an unreliable one-cylinder engine. The fairly ancient half-brother was the only one who could make the engine go at all. It was extremely difficult to start, and he always had to unscrew the sparking-plug and pour petrol into the cylinder. Then he swung a flywheel round and round, and with a bit of luck, after a lot of coughing and spluttering, the thing would finally get going.

When we first acquired the motor-boat, my youngest sister was four and I was seven, and by then all of us had learnt to swim. The exciting new boat made it possible for us to go much farther afield, and every day we would travel far out into the fjord, hunting for a different island. There were hundreds of them to choose from. Some were very small, no more than thirty yards long. Others were quite large, maybe half a mile in length. It was wonderful to have such a choice of places, and it was terrific fun to explore each island before we went swimming off the rocks. There were the wooden skeletons of ship-wrecked boats on those islands, and big white bones (were they human bones?), and wild raspberries, and mussels clinging to the rocks, and some of the islands had shaggy long-haired goats on them, and even sheep.

Now and again, when we were out in the open water beyond the chain of islands, the sea became very rough, and that was when my mother enjoyed herself most.

Nobody, not even the tiny children, bothered with life-belts in those days. We would cling to the sides of our funny little white motor-boat, driving through mountainous white-capped waves and getting drenched to the skin, while my mother calmly handled the tiller. There were times, I promise you, when the waves were so high that as we slid down into a trough the whole world disappeared from sight. Then up and up the little boat would climb, standing almost vertically on its tail, until we reached the crest of the next wave, and then it was like being on top of a foaming mountain. It requires great skill to handle a small boat in seas like these. The thing can easily capsize or be swamped if the bows do not meet the great combing breakers at just the right angle. But my mother knew exactly how to do it, and we were never afraid. We loved every minute of it, all of us except for our long-suffering Nanny, who would bury her face in her hands and call aloud upon the Lord to save her soul.

In the early evenings we nearly always went out fishing. We collected mussels from the rocks for bait, then we got into either the row-boat or the motor-boat and pushed off to drop anchor later in some likely spot. The water was very deep and often we had to let out two hundred feet of line before we touched bottom. We would sit silent and tense, waiting for a bite, and it always amazed me how even a little nibble at the end of that long line would be transmitted to one's fingers. 'A bite!' someone would shout, jerking the line. 'I've got him! It's a big one! It's a whopper!' And then came the thrill of hauling in the line hand over hand and peering over the side into the clear water to see how big the fish really was as he neared the surface. Cod, whiting, haddock and mackerel, we caught them all and bore them back triumphantly to the hotel kitchen where the cheery fat woman who did the cooking promised to get them ready for our supper.

I tell you, my friends, those were the days.

A visit to the doctor

I have only one unpleasant memory of the summer holidays in Norway. We were in the grandparents' house in Oslo and my mother said to me, 'We are going to the doctor this afternoon. He wants to look at your nose and mouth.'

I think I was eight at the time. 'What's wrong with my nose and mouth?' I asked.

'Nothing much,' my mother said. 'But I think you've got adenoids.'

'What are *they*?' I asked her.

'Don't worry about it,' she said. 'It's nothing.'

I held my mother's hand as we walked to the doctor's house. It took us about half an hour. There was a kind of dentist's chair in the surgery and I was lifted into it. The doctor had a round mirror strapped to his forehead and he peered up my nose and into my mouth. He then took my mother aside and they held a whispered conversation. I saw my mother looking rather grim, but she nodded.

The doctor now put some water to boil in an aluminium mug over a gas flame, and into the boiling water he placed a long thin shiny steel instrument. I sat there watching the steam coming off the boiling water. I was not in the least apprehensive. I was too young to realize that something out of the ordinary was going to happen.

Then a nurse dressed in white came in. She was carrying a red rubber apron and a curved white enamel bowl. She put the apron over the front of my body and tied it around my neck. It was far too big. Then she held the enamel bowl under my chin. The curve of the bowl fitted perfectly against the curve of my chest.

The doctor was bending over me. In his hand he held that long shiny steel instrument. He held it right in front of my face, and to this day I can still describe it perfectly. It was about the thickness and length of a pencil, and like most pencils it had a lot of sides to it. Toward the end, the metal became much thinner, and at the very end of the thin bit of metal there was a tiny blade set at an angle. The blade wasn't more than a centimetre long, very small, very sharp and very shiny.

'Open your mouth,' the doctor said, speaking Norwegian.

I refused. I thought he was going to do something to my teeth, and everything anyone had ever done to my teeth had been painful.

'It won't take two seconds,' the doctor said. He spoke gently, and I was seduced by his voice. Like an ass, I opened my mouth.

The tiny blade flashed in the bright light and disappeared into my mouth. It went high up into the roof of my mouth, and the hand that held the blade gave four or five very quick little twists and the next moment, out of my mouth into the basin came tumbling a whole mass of flesh and blood.

I was too shocked and outraged to do anything but yelp. I was horrified by the huge red lumps that had fallen out of my mouth into the white basin and my first thought was that the doctor had cut out the whole of the middle of my head.

'Those were your adenoids,' I heard the doctor saying.

I sat there gasping. The roof of my mouth seemed to be on fire. I grabbed my mother's hand and held on to it tight. I couldn't believe that anyone would do this to me.

'Stay where you are,' the doctor said. 'You'll be all right in a minute.'

Blood was still coming out of my mouth and dripping into the basin the nurse was holding. 'Spit it all out,' she said, 'there's a good boy.'

'You'll be able to breathe much better through your nose after this,' the doctor said.

The nurse wiped my lips and washed my face with a wet flannel. Then they lifted me out of the chair and stood me on my feet. I felt a bit groggy.

'We'll get you home,' my mother said, taking my hand. Down the stairs we went and on to the street. We started walking. I said *walking*. No trolley-car or taxi. We walked the full half-hour journey back to my grandparents' house, and when we arrived at last, I can remember as clearly as anything my grandmother saying, 'Let him sit down in that chair and rest for a while. After all, he's had an operation.'

Someone placed a chair for me beside my grandmother's armchair, and I sat down. My grandmother reached over and covered one of my hands in both of hers. 'That won't be the last time you'll go to a doctor in your life,' she said. 'And with a bit of luck, they won't do you too much harm.'

That was in 1924, and taking out a child's adenoids, and often the tonsils as well, without any anaesthetic was common practice in those days. I wonder, though, what you would think if some doctor did that to you today.

St Peter's,
1925–9
(age 9–13)

St. Peters uniform

Jack Hobbs
Cumberland Lodge Llandaff

Duckworth Butterflies my house
St. Peters
me in front row

Asta Else Alfhild me
Cardiff 1927

First day

In September 1925, when I was just nine, I set out on the first great adventure of my life – boarding-school. My mother had chosen for me a Prep School in a part of England which was as near as it could possibly be to our home in South Wales, and it was called St Peter's. The full postal address was St Peter's School, Weston-super-Mare, Somerset.

Weston-super-Mare is a slightly seedy seaside resort with a vast sandy beach, a tremendous long pier, an esplanade running along the sea-front, a clutter of hotels and boarding-houses, and about ten thousand little shops selling buckets and spades and sticks of rock and ice-creams. It lies almost directly across the Bristol Channel from Cardiff, and on a clear day you can stand on the esplanade at Weston and look across the fifteen or so miles of water and see the coast of Wales lying pale and milky on the horizon.

In those days the easiest way to travel from Cardiff to Weston-super-Mare was by boat. Those boats were beautiful. They were paddle-steamers, with gigantic swishing paddle-wheels on their flanks, and the wheels made the most terrific noise as they sloshed and churned through the water.

On the first day of my first term I set out by taxi in the

73

afternoon with my mother to catch the paddle-steamer from Cardiff Docks to Weston-super-Mare. Every piece of clothing I wore was brand new and had my name on it. I wore black shoes, grey woollen stockings with blue turn-overs, grey flannel shorts, a grey shirt, a red tie, a grey flannel blazer with the blue school crest on the breast pocket and a grey school cap with the same crest just above the peak. Into the taxi that was taking us to the docks went my brand new trunk and my brand new tuck-box, and both had R. DAHL painted on them in black.

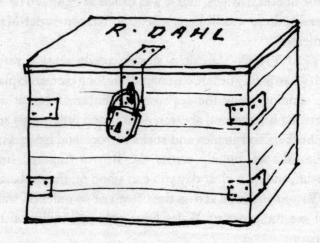

A tuck-box is a small pine wood trunk which is very strongly made, and no boy has ever gone as a boarder to an English Prep School without one. It is his own secret store-house, as secret as a lady's handbag, and there is an unwritten law that no other boy, no teacher, not even the Headmaster himself has the right to pry into the contents of your tuck-box. The owner has the key in his pocket and that is where it stays. At St Peter's, the tuck-boxes were ranged shoulder to shoulder all around the four walls of the changing-room and your own tuck-box stood directly below the peg on which you hung your games clothes. A tuck-box, as the name implies, is a box in which you store your tuck. At Prep School in those days, a parcel of tuck was sent once a week by anxious mothers to their ravenous little sons, and an average tuck-box would probably contain, at almost any time, half a home-made currant cake, a packet of squashed-fly biscuits, a couple of oranges, an apple, a banana, a pot of strawberry jam or Marmite, a bar of chocolate, a bag of Liquorice Allsorts and a tin of Bassett's lemonade powder. An English school in those days was purely a money-making business owned and operated by the Headmaster. It suited him, therefore, to give the boys as little food as possible himself and to encourage the parents in various cunning ways to feed their offspring by parcel-post from home.

'By all means, my dear Mrs Dahl, do send your boy some little treats now and again,' he would say. 'Perhaps a few oranges and apples once a week' – fruit was very expensive – 'and a nice currant cake, a *large* currant cake perhaps because small boys have large appetites do they not, ha-ha-ha ... Yes, yes, as *often* as you like. *More* than once a week if you wish ... *Of course* he'll be getting plenty of good food here, the best there is, but it never tastes *quite* the same as home cooking, does it? I'm sure you wouldn't want him to be the only one who doesn't get a lovely parcel from home every week.'

As well as tuck, a tuck-box would also contain all manner of treasures such as a magnet, a pocket-knife, a compass, a ball of string, a clockwork racing-car, half a dozen lead soldiers, a box of conjuring-tricks, some tiddlywinks, a Mexican jumping bean, a catapult, some foreign stamps, a couple of stink-bombs, and I remember one boy called Arkle who drilled an airhole in the lid of his tuckbox and kept a pet frog in there which he fed on slugs.

So off we set, my mother and I and my trunk and my tuck-box, and we boarded the paddle-steamer and went swooshing across the Bristol Channel in a shower of spray. I liked that part of it, but I began to grow apprehensive as I disembarked on to the pier at Weston-super-Mare and watched my trunk and tuck-box being loaded into an English taxi which would drive us to St Peter's. I had absolutely no idea what was in store for me. I had never spent a single night away from our large family before.

St Peter's was on a hill above the town. It was a long three-storeyed stone building that looked rather like a private lunatic asylum, and in front of it lay the playing-fields with their three football pitches. One-third of the building was reserved for the Headmaster and his family. The rest of it housed the boys, about one hundred and fifty of them altogether, if I remember rightly.

As we got out of the taxi, I saw the whole driveway abustle with small boys and their parents and their trunks and their tuck-boxes, and a man I took to be the Headmaster was swimming around among them shaking everybody by the hand.

I have already told you that *all* Headmasters are giants, and this one was no exception. He advanced upon my mother and shook her by the hand, then he shook me by the hand and as he did so he gave me the kind of flashing

the Loony Bin!

grin a shark might give to a small fish just before he gobbles it up. One of his front teeth, I noticed, was edged all the way round with gold, and his hair was slicked down with so much hair-cream that it glistened like butter.

'Right,' he said to me. 'Off you go and report to the Matron.' And to my mother he said briskly, 'Goodbye, Mrs Dahl. I shouldn't linger if I were you. We'll look after him.'

My mother got the message. She kissed me on the cheek and said goodbye and climbed right back into the taxi.

The Headmaster moved away to another group and I was left standing there beside my brand new trunk and my brand new tuck-box. I began to cry.

Writing home

At St Peter's, Sunday morning was letter-writing time. At nine o'clock the whole school had to go to their desks and spend one hour writing a letter home to their parents. At ten-fifteen we put on our caps and coats and formed up outside the school in a long crocodile and marched a couple of miles down into Weston-super-Mare for church, and we didn't get back until lunchtime. Church-going never became a habit with me. Letter-writing did.

Here is the very first letter I wrote home from St Peter's.

Dear Mama   23ᵗʰ Sept

I am having a lovely time here.
We play foot ball every day here. The
beds have no springs. Will you send my
stamp album, and quite a lot of swops.
The masters are very nice. I've
got all my clothes now, and and a belt,
and, ties, and a school Jersy.
            love from
                Boy

From that very first Sunday at St Peter's until the day my mother died thirty-two years later, I wrote to her once a week, sometimes more often, whenever I was away from home. I wrote to her every week from St Peter's (I had to), and every week from my next school, Repton, and every week from Dar es Salaam in East Africa, where I went on my first job after leaving school, and then every week during the war from Kenya and Iraq and Egypt when I was flying with the RAF.

... Major Cottam is going To recite something caled "as you like it" To night. Plese could you send me some conkers as quick as you can, but dont dont send To meny, the Just send them in a Tin and wrap it up in paper

My mother, for her part, kept every one of these letters, binding them carefully in neat bundles with green tape, but this was her own secret. She never told me she was doing it. In 1967, when she knew she was dying, I was in hospital in Oxford having a serious operation on my spine and I was unable to write to her. So she had a telephone specially installed beside her bed in order that she might have one last conversation with me. She didn't tell me she was dying nor did anyone else for that matter because I was in a fairly serious condition myself at the time. She simply asked me how I was and hoped I would get better soon and sent me her love. I had no idea that she would die the next day, but *she* knew all right and she wanted to reach out and speak to me for the last time.

When I recovered and went home, I was given this vast collection of my letters, all so neatly bound with green tape, more than six hundred of them altogether, dating from 1925 to 1945, each one in its original envelope with the old stamps still on them. I am awfully lucky to have something like this to refer to in my old age.

Letter-writing was a serious business at St Peter's. It was as much a lesson in spelling and punctuation as anything else because the Headmaster would patrol the classrooms all through the sessions, peering over our shoulders to read what we were writing and to point out our mistakes. But that, I am quite sure, was not the main reason for his interest. He was there to make sure that we said nothing horrid about his school.

> This is my Christmas wish list, as far as I can see.
>   a mashie-niblick, (which I have to close).
>   a decent book.
> I cant think of any thing else: If you send me a catalogue
> I might be able to tell you.

There was no way, therefore, that we could ever complain to our parents about anything during term-time. If we thought the food was lousy or if we hated a certain master or if we had been thrashed for something we did not do, we never dared to say so in our letters. In fact, we often went the other way. In order to please that dangerous Headmaster who was leaning over our shoulders and reading what we had written, we would say splendid things about the school and go on about how lovely the masters were.

> . a man called Mr
> Nichell gave us a fine lecture last knight on birds, he told
> us how owls eat mice they eat the hole mouse shin
> and all, and then all the shin and bones goes into a sort of
> little parcel in side him and he puts it on the ground, and
> those are caled pelets, and he showed us some pictures of some
> witch he has found, and of lots of other Birds.

Mind you, the Headmaster was a clever fellow. He did not want our parents to think that those letters of ours were censored in this way, and therefore he never allowed us to correct a spelling mistake in the letter itself. If, for example, I had written . . . *last Tuesday knight we had a lecture* . . ., he would say:

'Don't you know how to spell night?'

'Y-yes, sir, k-n-i-g-h-t.'

'That's the other kind of knight, you idiot!'

'Which kind, sir? I . . . I don't understand.'

'The one in shining armour! The man on horseback!' How do you spell Tuesday night?'

'I . . . I . . . I'm not quite sure, sir.'

'It's n-i-g-h-t, boy, n-i-g-h-t. Stay in and write it out for me fifty times this afternoon. No, no! Don't change it in the letter! You don't want to make it any messier than it is! It must go as you wrote it!'

Thus, the unsuspecting parents received in this subtle way the impression that your letter had never been seen or censored or corrected by anyone.

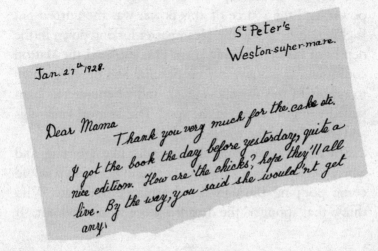

St Peter's
Weston-super-mare.

Jan. 27th 1928.

Dear Mama

Thank you very much for the cake etc. I got the book the day before yesterday; quite a nice edition. How are 'the chicks? hope they'll all live. By the way, you said she would'nt get any.

The Matron

At St Peter's the ground floor was all classrooms. The first floor was all dormitories. On the dormitory floor the Matron ruled supreme. This was her territory. Hers was the only voice of authority up here, and even the eleven- and twelve-year-old boys were terrified of this female ogre, for she ruled with a rod of steel.

The Matron was a large fair-haired woman with a bosom. Her age was probably no more than twenty-eight but it made no difference whether she was twenty-eight or sixty-eight because to us a grown-up was a grown-up and all grown-ups were dangerous creatures at this school.

Once you had climbed to the top of the stairs and set foot on the dormitory floor, you were in the Matron's power, and the source of this power was the unseen but frightening figure of the Headmaster lurking down in the depths of his study below. At any time she liked, the Matron could send you down in your pyjamas and dressing-gown to report to this merciless giant, and whenever this happened you got caned on the spot. The Matron knew this and she relished the whole business.

She could move along that corridor like lightning, and when you least expected it, her head and her bosom would come popping through the dormitory doorway. 'Who threw that sponge?' the dreaded voice would call out. 'It was *you*, Perkins, was it not? Don't lie to me, Perkins! Don't argue with me! I know perfectly well it was you! Now you can put your dressing-gown on and go downstairs and report to the Headmaster this instant!'

In slow motion and with immense reluctance, little Perkins, aged eight and a half, would get into his dressing-gown and slippers and disappear down the long corridor that led to the back stairs and the Headmaster's private quarters. And the Matron, as we all knew, would follow after him and stand at the top of the stairs listening with a funny look on her face for the *crack . . . crack . . . crack* of the cane that would soon be coming up from below. To me that noise always sounded as though the Headmaster was firing a pistol at the ceiling of his study.

Looking back on it now, there seems little doubt that the Matron disliked small boys very much indeed. She never smiled at us or said anything nice, and when for example the lint stuck to the cut on your kneecap, you were not allowed to take it off yourself bit by bit so that it didn't hurt. She would always whip it off with a flourish, muttering, 'Don't be such a ridiculous little baby!'

'We've got a new matron. Last term, one night in the washing room, having inspected a boy called Ford she kissed him and ~
We..

On one occasion during my first term, I went down to the Matron's room to have some iodine put on a grazed knee and I didn't know you had to knock before you entered. I opened the door and walked right in, and there she was in the centre of the Sick Room floor locked in some kind of an embrace with the Latin master, Mr Victor Corrado. They flew apart as I entered and both their faces went suddenly crimson.

'How *dare* you come in without knocking!' the Matron shouted. 'Here I am trying to get something out of Mr Corrado's eye and in you burst and disturb the whole delicate operation!'

'I'm very sorry, Matron.'

'Go away and come back in five minutes!' she cried, and I shot out of the room like a bullet.

After 'lights out' the Matron would prowl the corridor like a panther trying to catch the sound of a whisper behind a dormitory door, and we soon learnt that her powers of hearing were so phenomenal that it was safer to keep quiet.

Once, after lights out, a brave boy called Wragg tiptoed out of our dormitory and sprinkled caster sugar all over the linoleum floor of the corridor. When Wragg returned and told us that the corridor had been successfully sugared from one end to the other, I began shivering with excitement. I lay there in the dark in my bed waiting and waiting for the Matron to go on the prowl. Nothing happened. Perhaps, I told myself, she is in her room taking another speck of dust out of Mr Victor Corrado's eye.

Suddenly, from far down the corridor came a resounding *crunch*! *Crunch crunch crunch* went the footsteps. It sounded as though a giant was walking on loose gravel.

Then we heard the high-pitched furious voice of the Matron in the distance. 'Who did this?' she was shrieking. 'How *dare* you do this!' She went crunching along the corridor flinging open all the dormitory doors and switching on all the lights. The intensity of her fury was frightening. 'Come along!' she cried out, marching with crunching steps up and down the corridor. 'Own up! I want the name of the filthy little boy who put down the sugar! Own up immediately! Step forward! Confess!'

'Don't own up,' we whispered to Wragg. 'We won't give you away!'

Wragg kept quiet. I didn't blame him for that. Had he owned up, it was certain his fate would have been a terrible and a bloody one.

Soon the Headmaster was summoned from below. The Matron, with steam coming out of her nostrils, cried out to him for help, and now the whole school was herded into the long corridor, where we stood freezing in our pyjamas and bare feet while the culprit or culprits were ordered to step forward.

Nobody stepped forward.

I could see that the Headmaster was getting very angry indeed. His evening had been interrupted. Red splotches were appearing all over his face and flecks of spit were shooting out of his mouth as he talked.

'Very well!' he thundered. 'Every one of you will go at once and get the key to his tuck-box! Hand the keys to Matron, who will keep them for the rest of the term! And all parcels coming from home will be confiscated from now on! I will not tolerate this kind of behaviour!'

We handed in our keys and throughout the remaining six weeks of the term we went very hungry. But all through those six weeks, Arkle continued to feed his frog with slugs through the hole in the lid of his tuck-box. Using an old teapot, he also poured water in through the hole every day to keep the creature moist and happy. I admired Arkle very much for looking after his frog so well. Although he himself was famished, he refused to let his frog go hungry. Ever since then I have tried to be kind to small animals.

Each dormitory had about twenty beds in it. These were smallish narrow beds ranged along the walls on either side. Down the centre of the dormitory stood the basins where you washed your hands and face and did your teeth, always with cold water which stood in large jugs on the floor. Once you had entered the dormitory, you were not allowed to leave it unless you were reporting to the Matron's room with some sickness or injury. Under each bed there was a white chamber-pot, and before getting into bed you were expected to kneel on the floor and empty your bladder into it. All around the dormitory, just before 'lights out', was heard the *tinkle-tinkle* of little boys peeing into their pots. Once you had done this and got into your bed, you were not allowed to get out of it again until next morning. There was, I believe, a lavatory somewhere along the corridor, but only an attack of acute diarrhoea would be accepted as an excuse for visiting it. A journey to the upstairs lavatory automatically classed you as a diarrhoea victim, and a dose of thick white liquid would immediately be forced down your throat by the Matron. This made you constipated for a week.

Thanks for your letter. There are exactly 23 boys with the measles and all the other schools (boys) in West have got it. Hope Louis hasn't had any thing else wrong

The first miserable homesick night at St Peter's, when I curled up in bed and the lights were put out, I could think of nothing but our house at home and my mother and my sisters. Where were they? I asked myself. In which direction from where I was lying was Llandaff? I began to work it out and it wasn't difficult to do this because I had the Bristol Channel to help me. If I looked out of the dormitory window I could see the Channel itself, and the big city of Cardiff with Llandaff alongside it lay almost directly across the water but slightly to the north. Therefore, if I turned towards the window I would be facing home. I wriggled round in my bed and faced my home and my family.

From then on, during all the time I was at St Peter's, I never went to sleep with my back to my family. Different beds in different dormitories required the working out of new directions, but the Bristol Channel was always my guide and I was always able to draw an imaginary line from my bed to our house over in Wales. Never once did I go to sleep looking away from my family. It was a great comfort to do this.

Do you know that a chap called Ford has got double Pneumonia on top of measles.!!!!!! we've all got to be like mice going up to bed.

There was a boy in our dormitory during my first term called Tweedie, who one night started snoring soon after he had gone to sleep.

'Who's that talking?' cried the Matron, bursting in. My own bed was close to the door, and I remember looking up at her from my pillow and seeing her standing there silhouetted against the light from the corridor and thinking how truly frightening she looked. I think it was her enormous bosom that scared me most of all. My eyes were riveted to it, and to me it was like a battering-ram or the bows of an icebreaker or maybe a couple of high-explosive bombs.

'Own up!' she cried. 'Who was talking?'

We lay there in silence. Then Tweedie, who was lying fast asleep on his back with his mouth open, gave another snore.

The Matron stared at Tweedie. 'Snoring is a disgusting habit,' she said. 'Only the lower classes do it. We shall have to teach him a lesson.'

She didn't switch on the light, but she advanced into the room and picked up a cake of soap from the nearest basin. The bare electric bulb in the corridor illuminated the whole dormitory in a pale creamy glow.

None of us dared to sit up in bed, but all eyes were on the Matron now, watching to see what she was going to do next. She always had a pair of scissors hanging by a white tape from her waist, and with this she began shaving thin slivers of soap into the palm of one hand. Then she went over to where the wretched Tweedie lay and very carefully she dropped these little soap-flakes into his open mouth. She had a whole handful of them and I thought she was never going to stop.

What on earth is going to happen? I wondered. Would Tweedie choke? Would he strangle? Might his throat get blocked up completely? Was she going to kill him?

The Matron stepped back a couple of paces and folded her arms across, or rather underneath, her massive chest.

Nothing happened. Tweedie kept right on snoring.

Then suddenly he began to gurgle and white bubbles appeared around his lips. The bubbles grew and grew until in the end his whole face seemed to be smothered in a bubbly foaming white soapy froth. It was a horrific sight. Then all at once, Tweedie gave a great cough and a splutter and he sat up very fast and began clawing at his face with his hands. 'Oh!' he stuttered. 'Oh! Oh! Oh! Oh no! Wh-wh-what's happening? Wh-wh-what's on my face? Somebody help me!'

The Matron threw him a face flannel and said, 'Wipe it off, Tweedie. And don't ever let me hear you snoring again. Hasn't anyone ever taught you not to go to sleep on your back?'

With that she marched out of the dormitory and slammed the door.

very bad, he got better on Friday but has again got very ill, Jord is still P.S. We have just been informed that poor little Jord died early this morning.

Homesickness

I was homesick during the whole of my first term at St Peter's. Homesickness is a bit like seasickness. You don't know how awful it is till you get it, and when you do, it hits you right in the top of the stomach and you want to die. The only comfort is that both homesickness and seasickness are instantly curable. The first goes away the moment you walk out of the school grounds and the second is forgotten as soon as the ship enters port.

I was so devastatingly homesick during my first two weeks that I set about devising a stunt for getting myself sent back home, even if it were only a few days. My idea was that I should all of a sudden develop an attack of acute appendicitis.

You will probably think it silly that a nine-year-old boy should imagine he could get away with a trick like that, but I had sound reasons for trying it on. Only a month before, my ancient half-sister, who was twelve years older than me, had actually *had* appendicitis, and for several days before her operation I was able to observe her behaviour at close quarters. I noticed that the thing she complained about most was a severe pain down in the lower right side of her tummy. As well as this, she kept being sick and refused to eat and ran a temperature.

You might, by the way, be interested to know that this

sister had her appendix removed not in a fine hospital operating-room full of bright lights and gowned nurses but on our own nursery table at home by the local doctor and his anaesthetist. In those days it was fairly common

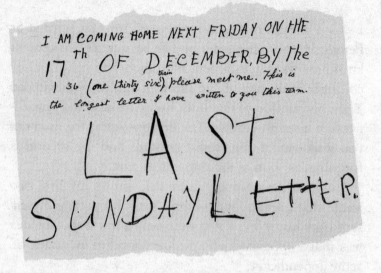

I AM COMING HOME NEXT FRIDAY ON THE 17th OF DECEMBER, BY the 1 36 (one thirty six) train please meet me. This is the longest letter I have written to you this term. LAST SUNDAY LETTER.

practice for a doctor to arrive at your own house with a bag of instruments, then drape a sterile sheet over the most convenient table and get on with it. On this occasion, I can remember lurking in the corridor outside the nursery while the operation was going on. My other sisters were with me, and we stood there spellbound, listening to the soft medical murmurs coming from behind the locked door and picturing the patient with her stomach sliced open like a lump of beef. We could even smell the sickly fumes of ether filtering through the crack under the door.

The next day, we were allowed to inspect the appendix itself in a glass bottle. It was a longish black wormy-looking thing, and I said, 'Do *I* have one of those inside me, Nanny?'

'Everybody has one,' Nanny answered.

'What's it for?' I asked her.

'God works in his mysterious ways,' she said, which was her stock reply whenever she didn't know the answer.

'What makes it go bad?' I asked her.

'Toothbrush bristles,' she answered, this time with no hesitation at all.

'*Toothbrush* bristles?' I cried. 'How can *toothbrush* bristles make your appendix go bad?'

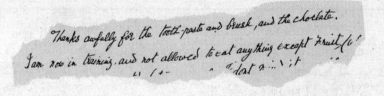

Nanny, who in my eyes was filled with more wisdom than Solomon, replied, 'Whenever a bristle comes out of your toothbrush and you swallow it, it sticks in your appendix and turns it rotten. In the war', she went on, 'the German spies used to sneak boxloads of loose-bristled toothbrushes into our shops and millions of our soldiers got appendicitis.'

'Honestly, Nanny?' I cried. 'Is that honestly true?'

'I never lie to you, child,' she answered. 'So let that be a lesson to you never to use an old toothbrush.'

For years after that, I used to get nervous whenever I found a toothbrush bristle on my tongue.

As I went upstairs and knocked on the brown door after breakfast, I didn't even feel frightened of the Matron.

'Come in!' boomed the voice.

I entered the room clutching my stomach on the right-hand side and staggering pathetically.

'What's the matter with you?' the Matron shouted, and the sheer force of her voice caused that massive bosom to quiver like a gigantic blancmange.

'It hurts, Matron,' I moaned. 'Oh, it hurts so much! Just here!'

'You've been over-eating!' she barked. 'What do you expect if you guzzle currant cake all day long!'

'I haven't eaten a thing for days,' I lied. 'I *couldn't* eat, Matron! I simply *couldn't*!'

'Get on the bed and lower your trousers,' she ordered.

I lay on the bed and she began prodding my tummy violently with her fingers. I was watching her carefully, and when she hit what I guessed was the appendix place, I let out a yelp that rattled the window-panes. 'Ow! Ow! Ow!' I cried out. 'Don't, Matron, don't!' Then I slipped in the clincher. 'I've been sick all morning,' I moaned, 'and now there's nothing left to be sick with, but I still feel sick!'

This was the right move. I saw her hesitate. 'Stay where you are,' she said and she walked quickly from the room. She may have been a foul and beastly woman, but she had

had a nurse's training and she didn't want a ruptured appendix on her hands.

Within an hour, the doctor arrived and he went through the same prodding and poking and I did my yelping at what I thought were the proper times. Then he put a thermometer in my mouth.

'Hmm,' he said. 'It reads normal. Let me feel your stomach once more.'

'Owch!' I screamed when he touched the vital spot.

The doctor went away with the Matron. The Matron returned half an hour later and said, 'The Headmaster has telephoned your mother and she's coming to fetch you this afternoon.'

I didn't answer her. I just lay there trying to look very ill, but my heart was singing out with all sorts of wonderful songs of praise and joy.

I was taken home across the Bristol Channel on the paddle-steamer and I felt so wonderful at being away from that dreaded school building that I very nearly forgot I was meant to be ill. That afternoon I had a session with Dr Dunbar at his surgery in Cathedral Road, Cardiff, and I tried the same tricks all over again. But Dr Dunbar was far wiser and more skilful than either the Matron or the school doctor. After he had prodded my stomach and I had done my yelping routine, he said to me, 'Now you can get dressed again and seat yourself on that chair.'

He himself sat down behind his desk and fixed me with a penetrating but not unkindly eye. 'You're faking, aren't you?' he said.

'How do you know?' I blurted out.

'Because your stomach is soft and perfectly normal,' he answered. 'If you had had an inflammation down there, the stomach would have been hard and rigid. It's quite easy to tell.'

I kept silent.

'I expect you're homesick,' he said.

I nodded miserably.

'Everyone is at first,' he said. 'You have to stick it out. And don't blame your mother for sending you away to boarding-school. She insisted you were too young to go, but it was I who persuaded her it was the right thing to do. Life is tough, and the sooner you learn how to cope with it the better for you.'

'What will you tell the school?' I asked him, trembling.

'I'll say you had a very severe infection of the stomach which I am curing with pills,' he answered smiling. 'It will mean that you must stay home for three more days. But promise me you won't try anything like this again. Your mother has enough on her hands, without having to rush over to fetch you out of school.'

'I promise,' I said. 'I'll never do it again.'

I'm taking the Calsium, but have'nt needed one of the Pills yet.

Somehow or other I got through the first term at St Peter's, and towards the end of December my mother came over on the paddle-boat to take me and my trunk home for the Christmas holidays.

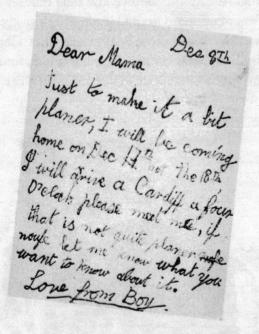

Dear Mama   Dec 9th

Just to make it a bit
planer, I will be coming
home on Dec 14th not the 18th
I will drive a Cardiff a four
O'clok please meet me, if
that is not quite planer nufe
noufe let me know what you
want to know about it.
Love from Boy

Oh the bliss and the wonder of being with the family once again after all those weeks of fierce discipline! Unless you have been to boarding-school when you are very young, it is absolutely impossible to appreciate the delights of living at home. It is almost *worth* going away because it's so lovely coming back. I could hardly believe that I didn't have to wash in cold water in the mornings or keep silent in the corridors, or say 'Sir' to every grown-up man I met, or use a chamber-pot in the bedroom, or get flicked with wet towels while naked in the changing-room, or eat porridge for breakfast that seemed to be full of little round lumpy grey sheep's-droppings, or walk all day long in perpetual fear of the long yellow cane that lay on top of the corner-cupboard in the Headmaster's study.

The weather was exceptionally mild that Christmas holiday and one amazing morning our whole family got ready to go for our first drive in the first motor-car we had

ever owned. This new motor-car was an enormous long black French automobile called a De Dion-Bouton which had a canvas roof that folded back. The driver was to be that twelve-years-older-than-me half-sister (now aged twenty-one) who had recently had her appendix removed.

She had received two full half-hour lessons in driving from the man who delivered the car, and in that enlightened year of 1925 this was considered quite sufficient. Nobody had to take a driving-test. You were your own judge of competence, and as soon as you felt you were ready to go, off you jolly well went.

As we all climbed into the car, our excitement was so intense we could hardly bear it.

'How fast will it go?' we cried out. 'Will it do fifty miles an hour?'

'It'll do sixty!' the ancient sister answered. Her tone was so confident and cocky it should have scared us to death, but it didn't.

'Oh, let's make it do sixty!' we shouted. 'Will you promise to take us up to sixty?'

'We shall probably go faster than that,' the sister announced, pulling on her driving-gloves and tying a scarf over her head in the approved driving-fashion of the period.

The canvas hood had been folded back because of the mild weather, converting the car into a magnificent open tourer. Up front, there were three bodies in all, the driver behind the wheel, my half-brother (aged eighteen) and one of my sisters (aged twelve). In the back seat there were four more of us, my mother (aged forty), two small sisters (aged eight and five) and myself (aged nine). Our machine possessed one very special feature which I don't think you see on the cars of today. This was a second windscreen in the back solely to keep the breeze off the faces of the back-seat passengers when the hood was down. It had a long centre section and two little end sections that could be angled backwards to deflect the wind.

We were all quivering with fear and joy as the driver let out the clutch and the great long black automobile leaned forward and stole into motion.

'Are you sure you know how to do it?' we shouted. 'Do you know where the brakes are?'

'Be quiet!' snapped the ancient sister. 'I've got to concentrate!'

Down the drive we went and out into the village of Llandaff itself. Fortunately there were very few vehicles on the roads in those days. Occasionally you met a small truck or a delivery-van and now and again a private car, but the danger of colliding with anything else was fairly remote so long as you kept the car on the road.

The splendid black tourer crept slowly through the village with the driver pressing the rubber bulb of the horn every time we passed a human being, whether it was the butcher-boy on his bicycle or just a pedestrian strolling on the pavement. Soon we were entering a countryside of green fields and high hedges with not a soul in sight.

'You didn't think I could do it, did you?' cried the ancient sister, turning round and grinning at us all.

'Now you keep your eyes on the road,' my mother said nervously.

'Go faster!' we shouted. 'Go on! Make her go faster! Put your foot down! We're only doing *fifteen miles an hour*!'

Spurred on by our shouts and taunts, the ancient sister began to increase the speed. The engine roared and the body vibrated. The driver was clutching the steering-wheel as though it were the hair of a drowning man, and we all watched the speedometer needle creeping up to twenty, then twenty-five, then thirty. We were probably doing about thirty-five miles an hour when we came suddenly to a sharpish bend in the road. The ancient sister, never having been faced with a situation like this before, shouted 'Help!' and slammed on the brakes and swung the wheel wildly round. The rear wheels locked and went into a fierce sideways skid, and then, with a marvellous crunch of mudguards, and metal, we went crashing into the hedge. The front passengers all shot through the front windscreen and the back passengers all shot through the back windscreen. Glass (there was no Triplex then) flew in all directions and so did we. My brother and one sister landed on the bonnet of the car, someone else was catapulted out on to the road and at least one small sister landed in the middle of the hawthorn hedge. But miraculously nobody was hurt very much except me. My nose had been cut almost clean off my face as I went through the rear windscreen and now it was hanging on only by a single small thread of skin. My mother disentangled herself from the scrimmage and grabbed a handkerchief from her purse. She clapped the dangling nose back into place fast and held it there.

Not a cottage or a person was in sight, let alone a

telephone. Some kind of bird started twittering in a tree farther down the road, otherwise all was silent.

My mother was bending over me in the rear seat and saying, 'Lean back and keep your head still.' To the ancient sister she said, 'Can you get this thing going again?'

The sister pressed the starter and to everyone's surprise, the engine fired.

'Back it out of the hedge,' my mother said. 'And hurry.'

The sister had trouble finding reverse gear. The cogs were grinding against one another with a fearful noise of tearing metal.

'I've never actually driven it backwards,' she admitted at last.

Everyone with the exception of the driver, my mother and me was out of the car and standing on the road. The noise of gear-wheels grinding against each other was terrible. It sounded as though a lawn-mower was being driven over hard rocks. The ancient sister was using bad words and going crimson in the face, but then my brother leaned his head over the driver's door and said, 'Don't you have to put your foot on the clutch?'

The harassed driver depressed the clutch-pedal and the gears meshed and one second later the great black beast leapt backwards out of the hedge and careered across the road into the hedge on the other side.

'Try to keep cool,' my mother said. 'Go forward slowly.'

At last the shattered motor-car was driven out of the second hedge and stood sideways across the road, blocking the highway. A man with a horse and cart now appeared on the scene and the man dismounted from his cart and walked across to our car and leaned over the rear door. He had a big drooping moustache and he wore a small black bowler-hat.

'You're in a fair old mess 'ere, ain't you?' he said to my mother.

'Can you drive a motor-car?' my mother asked him.

'Nope,' he said. 'And you're blockin' up the 'ole road. I've got a thousand fresh-laid heggs in this cart and I want to get 'em to market before noon.'

'Get out of the way,' my mother told him. 'Can't you see there's a child in here who's badly injured?'

'One thousand fresh-laid heggs,' the man repeated, staring straight at my mother's hand and the blood-soaked handkerchief and the blood running down her wrist. 'And if I don't get 'em to market by noon today I won't be able to sell 'em till next week. Then they won't be fresh-laid any more, will they? I'll be stuck with one thousand stale ole heggs that nobody wants.'

'I hope they all go rotten,' my mother said. 'Now back that cart out of our way this instant!' And to the children standing on the road she cried out, 'Jump back into the car! We're going to the doctor!'

'There's glass all over the seats!' they shouted.

'Never mind the glass!' my mother said. 'We've got to get this boy to the doctor fast!'

The passengers crawled back into the car. The man with the horse and cart backed off to a safe distance. The ancient sister managed to straighten the vehicle and get it pointed in the right direction, and then at last the once magnificent automobile tottered down the highway and headed for Dr Dunbar's surgery in Cathedral Road, Cardiff.

'I've never driven in a city,' the ancient and trembling sister announced.

'You are about to do so,' my mother said. 'Keep going.'

Proceeding at no more than four miles an hour all the way, we finally made it to Dr Dunbar's house. I was hustled out of the car and in through the front door with my mother still holding the bloodstained handerchief firmly over my wobbling nose.

'Good heavens!' cried Dr Dunbar. 'It's been cut clean off!'

'It hurts,' I moaned.

'He can't go round without a nose for the rest of his life!' the doctor said to my mother.

'It looks as though he may have to,' my mother said.

'Nonsense!' the doctor told her. 'I shall sew it on again.'

'Can you do that?' My mother asked him.

'I can try,' he answered. 'I shall tape it on tight for now and I'll be up at your house with my assistant within the hour.'

Huge strips of sticking-plaster were strapped across my face to hold the nose in position. Then I was led back into the car and we crawled the two miles home to Llandaff.

About an hour later I found myself lying upon that same nursery table my ancient sister had occupied some months before for her appendix operation. Strong hands held me down while a mask stuffed with cotton-wool was clamped over my face. I saw a hand above me holding a bottle with white liquid in it and the liquid was being poured on to the cotton-wool inside the mask. Once again I smelled the sickly stench of chloroform and ether, and a voice was saying, 'Breathe deeply. Take some nice deep breaths.'

I fought fiercely to get off that table but my shoulders were pinned down by the full weight of a large man. The hand that was holding the bottle above my face kept tilting it farther and farther forward and the white liquid dripped and dripped on to the cotton-wool. Blood-red circles began to appear before my eyes and the circles started to spin round and round until they made a scarlet whirlpool with a deep black hole in the centre, and miles away in the distance a voice was saying, 'That's a good boy. We're nearly there now . . . we're nearly there . . . just close your eyes and go to sleep . . .'

I woke up in my own bed with my anxious mother sitting beside me, holding my hand. 'I didn't think you were ever going to come round,' she said. 'You've been asleep for more than eight hours.'

'Did Dr Dunbar sew my nose on again?' I asked her.

'Yes,' she said.

'Will it stay on?'

'He says it will. How do you feel, my darling?'

'Sick,' I said.

After I had vomited into a small basin, I felt a little better.

'Look under your pillow,' my mother said, smiling.

I turned and lifted a corner of my pillow, and underneath it, on the snow-white sheet, there lay a beautiful golden sovereign with the head of King George V on its uppermost side.

'That's for being brave,' my mother said. 'You did very well. I'm proud of you.'

Captain Hardcastle

We called them masters in those days, not teachers, and at St Peter's the one I feared most of all, apart from the Headmaster, was Captain Hardcastle.

This man was slim and wiry and he played football. On the football field he wore white running shorts and white gymshoes and short white socks. His legs were as hard and thin as ram's legs and the skin around his calves was almost exactly the colour of mutton fat. The hair on his head was not ginger. It was a brilliant dark vermilion, like a ripe orange, and it was plastered back with immense quantities of brilliantine in the same fashion as the Headmaster's. The parting in his hair was a white line straight down the middle of the scalp, so straight it could only have been made with a ruler. On either side of the parting you could see the comb tracks running back through the greasy orange hair like little tramlines.

Captain Hardcastle sported a moustache that was the same colour as his hair, and oh what a moustache it was! A truly terrifying sight, a thick orange hedge that sprouted and flourished between his nose and his upper lip and ran clear across his face from the middle of one cheek to the middle of the other. But this was not one of those nail-brush moustaches, all short and clipped and bristly. Nor was it long and droopy in the walrus style. Instead, it was curled most splendidly upwards all the way along as though it had had a permanent wave put into it or possibly curling tongs heated in the mornings over a tiny flame of methylated spirits. The only other way he could have achieved this curling effect, we boys decided, was by prolonged upward brushing with a hard toothbrush in front of the looking-glass every morning.

Behind the moustache there lived an inflamed and savage face with a deeply corrugated brow that indicated a very limited intelligence. 'Life is a puzzlement,' the corrugated brow seemed to be saying, 'and the world is a dangerous place. All men are enemies and small boys are insects that will turn and bite you if you don't get them first and squash them hard.'

Captain Hardcastle was never still. His orange head twitched and jerked perpetually from side to side in the most alarming fashion, and each twitch was accompanied by a little grunt that came out of the nostrils. He had been a soldier in the army in the Great War and that, of course, was how he had received his title. But even small insects like us knew that 'Captain' was not a very exalted rank and only a man with little else to boast about would hang on to it in civilian life. It was bad enough to keep calling your-self 'Major' after it was all over, but 'Captain' was the bottoms.

Rumour had it that the constant twitching and jerking and snorting was caused by something called shell-shock, but we were not quite sure what that was. We took it to mean that an explosive object had gone off very close to him with such an enormous bang that it had made him jump high in the air and he hadn't stopped jumping since.

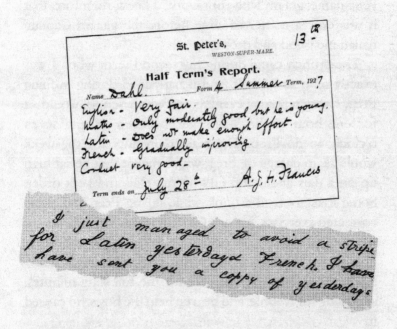

For a reason that I could never properly understand, Captain Hardcastle had it in for me from my very first day at St Peter's. Perhaps it was because he taught Latin and I was no good at it. Perhaps it was because already, at the age of nine, I was very nearly as tall as he was. Or even more likely, it was because I took an instant dislike to his giant orange moustache and he often caught me staring at it with what was probably a little sneer under the nose. I had only to pass within ten feet of him in the corridor and he would glare at me and shout, 'Hold yourself straight, boy! Pull your shoulders back!' or 'Take those hands out of your pockets!' or 'What's so funny, may I ask? What are you smirking at?' or most insulting of all, 'You, what's-your-name, get on with your work!' I knew, therefore, that it was only a matter of time before the gallant Captain nailed me good and proper.

The crunch came during my second term when I was exactly nine and a half, and it happened during evening Prep. Every weekday evening, the whole school would sit for one hour in the Main Hall, between six and seven o'clock, to do Prep. The master on duty for the week would be in charge of Prep, which meant that he sat high up on a dais at the top end of the Hall and kept order. Some masters read a book while taking Prep and some corrected exercises, but not Captain Hardcastle. He would sit up there on the dais twitching and grunting and never once would he look down at his desk. His small milky-blue eyes would rove the Hall for the full sixty minutes, searching for trouble, and heaven help the boy who caused it.

The rules of Prep were simple but strict. You were forbidden to look up from your work, and you were forbidden to talk. That was all there was to it, but it left you precious little leeway. In extreme circumstances, and I never knew what these were, you could put your hand up and wait until you were asked to speak but you had better be awfully sure that the circumstances were extreme. Only twice during my four years at St Peter's did I see a boy putting up his hand during Prep. The first one went like this:

MASTER. What is it?

BOY. Please sir, may I be excused to go to the lavatory?

MASTER. Certainly not. You should have gone before.

BOY. But sir . . . please sir . . . I didn't want to before . . . I didn't know . . .

MASTER. Whose fault was that? Get on with your work!

BOY. But sir . . . Oh sir . . . Please sir, let me go!

MASTER. One more word out of you and you'll be in trouble.

Naturally, the wretched boy dirtied his pants, which caused a storm later on upstairs with the Matron.

On the second occasion, I remember clearly that it was a summer term and the boy who put his hand up was called Braithwaite. I also seem to recollect that the master taking Prep was our friend Captain Hardcastle, but I wouldn't swear to it. The dialogue went something like this:

MASTER. Yes, what is it?

BRAITHWAITE. Please sir, a wasp came in through the window and it's stung me on my lip and it's swelling up.

MASTER. A *what*?

BRAITHWAITE. A wasp, sir.

MASTER. Speak up, boy, I can't hear you! A *what* came in through the window?

BRAITHWAITE. It's hard to speak up, sir, with my lip all swelling up.

MASTER. With your *what* all swelling up? Are you trying to be funny?

BRAITHWAITE. No sir, I promise I'm not sir.

MASTER. Talk properly, boy! What's the matter with you?

BRAITHWAITE. I've told you, sir. I've been stung, sir. My lip is swelling. It's hurting terribly.

MASTER. *Hurting terribly?* What's hurting terribly?

BRAITHWAITE. My lip, sir. It's getting bigger and bigger.

MASTER. What Prep are you doing tonight?

BRAITHWAITE. French verbs, sir. We have to write them out.

MASTER. Do you write with your lip?

BRAITHWAITE. No, sir, I don't sir, but you see . . .

MASTER. All I see is that you are making an infernal noise and disturbing everybody in the room. Now get on with your work.

They were tough, those masters, make no mistake about it, and if you wanted to survive, you had to become pretty tough yourself.

My own turn came, as I said, during my second term and Captain Hardcastle was again taking Prep. You should know that during Prep every boy in the Hall sat at his own small individual wooden desk. These desks had the usual sloping wooden tops with a narrow flat strip at the far end where there was a groove to hold your pen and a small hole in the right-hand side in which the ink-well sat. The pens we used had detachable nibs and it was necessary to dip your nib into the ink-well every six or seven seconds when you were writing. Ball-point pens and felt pens had not then been invented, and fountain-pens were forbidden. The nibs we used were very fragile and most boys kept a supply of new ones in a small box in their trouser pockets.

Prep was in progress. Captain Hardcastle was sitting up on the dais in front of us, stroking his orange moustache, twitching his head and grunting through his nose. His eyes roved the Hall endlessly, searching for mischief. The only noises to be heard were Captain Hardcastle's little snorting grunts and the soft sound of pen-nibs moving over paper. Occasionally there was a *ping* as somebody dipped his nib too violently into his tiny white porcelain ink-well.

Disaster struck when I foolishly stubbed the tip of my nib into the top of the desk. The nib broke. I knew I hadn't got a spare one in my pocket, but a broken nib was never accepted as an excuse for not finishing Prep. We had been set an essay to write and the subject was 'The Life Story of a Penny' (I still have that essay in my files). I had made a decent start and I was rattling along fine when I broke that nib. There was still another half-hour of Prep to go and I couldn't sit there doing nothing all that time. Nor could I put up my hand and tell Captain Hardcastle I had broken my nib. I simply did not dare. And as a matter of fact, I really *wanted* to finish that essay. I knew exactly what was going to happen to my penny through the next two pages and I couldn't bear to leave it unsaid.

I glanced to my right. The boy next to me was called Dobson. He was the same age as me, nine and a half, and

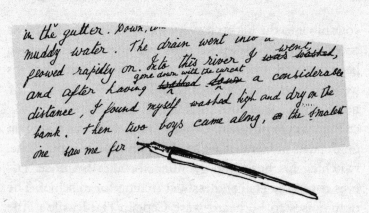

in the gutter. Down, w---
muddy water. The drain went into a
flowed rapidly on. Into this river I was washed, went,
and after having washed down a considerable gone down with the current
distance, I found myself washed high and dry on the
bank. Then two boys came along, as the smallest
one saw me fir ➤

a nice fellow. Even now, sixty years later, I can still remember that Dobson's father was a doctor and that he lived, as I had learnt from the label on Dobson's tuck-box, at The Red House, Uxbridge, Middlesex.

Dobson's desk was almost touching mine. I thought I would risk it. I kept my head lowered but watched Captain Hardcastle very carefully. When I was fairly sure he was looking the other way, I put a hand in front of my mouth and whispered, 'Dobson ... Dobson ... Could you lend me a nib?'

Suddenly there was an explosion up on the dais. Captain Hardcastle had leapt to his feet and was pointing at me and shouting, 'You're talking! I saw you talking! Don't try to deny it! I distinctly saw you talking behind your hand!'

I sat there frozen with terror.

Every boy stopped working and looked up.

Captain Hardcastle's face had gone from red to deep purple and he was twitching violently.

'Do you deny you were talking?' he shouted.

'No, sir, no, b-but . . .'

'And do you deny you were trying to cheat? Do you deny you were asking Dobson for help with your work?'

'N-no, sir, I wasn't. I wasn't cheating.'

'Of course you were cheating! Why else, may I ask, would you be speaking to Dobson? I take it you were not inquiring after his health?'

It is worth reminding the reader once again of my age. I was not a self-possessed lad of fourteen. Nor was I twelve or even ten years old. I was nine and a half, and at that age one is ill equipped to tackle a grown-up man with flaming orange hair and a violent temper. One can do little else but stutter.

'I . . . I have broken my nib, sir,' I whispered. 'I . . . I was asking Dobson if he c-could lend me one, sir.'

'You are lying!' cried Captain Hardcastle, and there was triumph in his voice. 'I always knew you were a liar! *And* a cheat as well!'

'All I w-wanted was a nib, sir.'

'I'd shut up if I were you!' thundered the voice on the dais. 'You'll only get yourself into deeper trouble! I am giving you a Stripe!'

These were words of doom. A Stripe! *I am giving you a Stripe!* All around, I could feel a kind of sympathy reaching out to me from every boy in the school, but nobody moved or made a sound.

Here I must explain the system of Stars and Stripes that we had at St Peter's. For exceptionally good work, you could be awarded a Quarter-Star, and a red dot was made with crayon beside your name on the notice-board. If you got four Quarter-Stars, a red line was drawn through the four dots indicating that you had completed your Star.

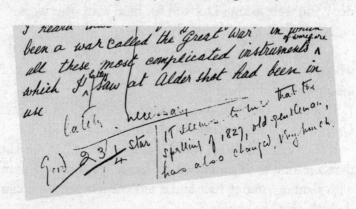

I heard ... been a war called the "Great" War in former of warfare all these most complicated instruments which I lately saw at Alder shot had been in use lately ... necessary ... Good 2 3/4 Star | It seems to me that the spelling of 1827, old gentleman, has also changed. Very much.

For exceptionally poor work or bad behaviour, you were given a Stripe, and that automatically meant a thrashing from the Headmaster.

Every master had a book of Quarter-Stars and a book of Stripes, and these had to be filled in and signed and torn out exactly like cheques from a cheque book. The Quarter-Stars were pink, the Stripes were a fiendish, blue-green colour. The boy who received a Star or a Stripe would pocket it until the following morning after prayers, when the Headmaster would call upon anyone who had been given one or the other to come forward in front of the whole school and hand it in. Stripes were considered so dreadful that they were not given very often. In any one week it was unusual for more than two or three boys to receive Stripes.

And now Captain Hardcastle was giving one to me.

'Come here,' he ordered.

I got up from my desk and walked to the dais. He already

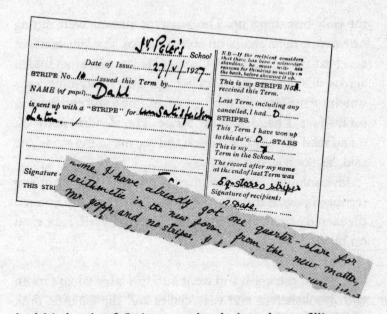

St Peter's School

Date of Issue .... 27/XI/ 1927 ...

STRIPE No. 10 ....Issued this Term by......

NAME (of pupil) ...Dahl

is sent up with a "STRIPE" for ...unsatisfactory
Latin ✓

Signature
THIS STRIP...

N.B.—If the recipient considers
that there has been a misunderstanding, he must write his
reasons for thinking so neatly on
the back, before showing it up.

This is my STRIPE No. ...
received this Term.

Last Term, including any
cancelled, I had... D
STRIPES.

This Term I have won up
to this da'e. O ....STARS

This is my ...
Term in the School.

The record after my name
at the end of last Term was

8 ½ Stars o stripes
Signature of recipient:
R Dahl

...me I have already got one quarter-stare for
arithmetic in the new form from the new master,
Mr. Jopp, and no stripes. ...

had his book of Stripes on the desk and was filling one
out. He was using red ink, and along the line where it said
Reason, he wrote, *Talking in Prep, trying to cheat and lying.* He
signed it and tore it out of the book. Then, taking plenty
of time, he filled in the counterfoil. He picked up the terrible piece of green-blue paper and waved it in my
direction but he didn't look up. I took it out of his hand
and walked back to my desk. The eyes of the whole school
followed my progress.

For the remainder of Prep I sat at my desk and did
nothing. Having no nib, I was unable to write another
word about 'The Life Story of a Penny', but I was made
to finish it the next afternoon instead of playing games.

The following morning, as soon as prayers were over,
the Headmaster called for Quarter-Stars and Stripes. I was

the only boy to go up. The assistant masters were sitting on very upright chairs on either side of the Headmaster, and I caught a glimpse of Captain Hardcastle, arms folded across his chest, head twitching, the milky-blue eyes watching me intently, the look of triumph still glimmering on his face. I handed in my Stripe. The Headmaster took it and read the writing. 'Come and see me in my study', he said, 'as soon as this is over.'

Five minutes later, walking on my toes and trembling terribly, I passed through the green baize door and entered the sacred precincts where the Headmaster lived. I knocked on his study door.

'Enter!'

I turned the knob and went into this large square room with bookshelves and easy chairs and the gigantic desk topped in red leather straddling the far corner. The Headmaster was sitting behind the desk holding my Stripe in his fingers. 'What have you got to say for yourself?' he asked me, and the white shark's teeth flashed dangerously between his lips.

'I didn't lie, sir,' I said. 'I promise I didn't. And I wasn't trying to cheat.'

'Captain Hardcastle says you were doing both,' the Headmaster said. 'Are you calling Captain Hardcastle a liar?'

'No, sir. Oh no, sir.'

'I wouldn't if I were you.'

'I had broken my nib, sir, and I was asking Dobson if he could lend me another.'

'That is not what Captain Hardcastle says. He says you were asking for help with your essay.'

'Oh no, sir, I wasn't. I was a long way away from Captain Hardcastle and I was only whispering. I don't think he could have heard what I said, sir.'

'So you *are* calling him a liar.'

'Oh no, sir! No, sir! I would never do that!'

It was impossible for me to win against the Headmaster. What I would like to have said was, 'Yes, sir, if you really want to know, sir, I *am* calling Captain Hardcastle a liar because that's what he is!', but it was out of the question. I did, however, have one trump card left to play, or I thought I did.

'You could ask Dobson, sir,' I whispered.

'*Ask Dobson?*' he cried. 'Why should I ask Dobson?'

'He would tell you what I said, sir.'

'Captain Hardcastle is an officer and a gentleman,' the Headmaster said. 'He has told me what happened. I hardly think I want to go round asking some silly little boy if Captain Hardcastle is speaking the truth.'

I kept silent.

'For talking in Prep,' the Headmaster went on, 'for trying to cheat and for lying, I am going to give you six strokes of the cane.'

He rose from his desk and crossed over to the corner-cupboard on the opposite side of the study. He reached up and took from the top of it three very thin yellow canes, each with the bent-over handle at one end. For a few seconds, he held them in his hands, examining them with some care, then he selected one and replaced the other two on top of the cupboard.

'Bend over.'

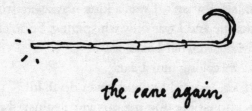

the cane again

I was frightened of that cane. There is no small boy in the world who wouldn't be. It wasn't simply an instrument for beating you. It was a weapon for wounding. It lacerated the skin. It caused severe black and scarlet bruising that took three weeks to disappear, and all the time during those three weeks, you could feel your heart beating along the wounds.

I tried once more, my voice slightly hysterical now. 'I didn't do it, sir! I swear I'm telling the truth!'

'Be quiet and bend over! Over there! And touch your toes!'

Very slowly, I bent over. Then I shut my eyes and braced myself for the first stroke.

Crack! It was like a rifle shot! With a very hard stroke of the cane on one's buttocks, the time-lag before you feel any pain is about four seconds. Thus, the experienced caner will always pause between strokes to allow the agony to reach its peak.

So for a few seconds after the first *crack* I felt virtually nothing. Then suddenly came the frightful searing agonizing unbearable burning across the buttocks, and as it reached its highest and most excruciating point, the second *crack* came down. I clutched hold of my ankles as tight as I could and I bit into my lower lip. I was determined not to make a sound, for that would only give the executioner greater satisfaction.

Crack! . . . Five seconds pause.

Crack! . . . Another pause.

Crack! . . . And another pause.

I was counting the strokes, and as the sixth one hit me, I knew I was going to survive in silence.

'That will do,' the voice behind me said.

I straightened up and clutched my backside as hard as I possibly could with both hands. This is always the instinctive and automatic reaction. The pain is so frightful you try to grab hold of it and tear it away, and the tighter you squeeze, the more it helps.

I did not look at the Headmaster as I hopped across the thick red carpet towards the door. The door was closed and nobody was about to open it for me, so for a couple of seconds I had to let go of my bottom with one hand to turn the door-knob. Then I was out and hopping around in the hallway of the private sanctum.

Directly across the hall from the Headmaster's study was the assistant masters' Common Room. They were all in there now waiting to spread out to their respective classrooms, but what I couldn't help noticing, even in my agony, was that *this door was open*.

Why was it open?

Had it been left that way on purpose so that they could all hear more clearly the sound of the cane from across the hall?

Of course it had. And I felt quite sure that it was Captain

Hardcastle who had opened it. I pictured him standing in there among his colleagues snorting with satisfaction at every stinging stroke.

Small boys can be very comradely when a member of their community has got into trouble, and even more so when they feel an injustice has been done. When I returned to the classroom, I was surrounded on all sides by sympathetic faces and voices, but one particular incident has always stayed with me. A boy of my own age called Highton was so violently incensed by the whole affair that he said to me before lunch that day, '*You* don't have a father. I do. I am going to write to my father and tell him what has happened and he'll do something about it.'

'He couldn't do anything,' I said.

'Oh yes he could,' Highton said. 'And what's more he will. My father won't let them get away with this.'

'Where is he now?'

'He's in Greece,' Highton said. 'In Athens. But that won't make any difference.'

Then and there, little Highton sat down and wrote to the father he admired so much, but of course nothing came of it. It was nevertheless a touching and generous gesture from one small boy to another and I have never forgotten it.

Little Ellis and the boil

During my third term at St Peter's, I got flu and was put to bed in the Sick Room, where the dreaded Matron reigned supreme. In the next bed to mine was a seven-year-old boy called Ellis, whom I liked a lot. Ellis was there because he had an immense and angry-looking boil on the inside of his thigh. I saw it. It was as big as a plum and about the same colour.

One morning, in came the doctor to examine us, and sailing along beside him was the Matron. Her mountainous bosom was enclosed in a starched white envelope, and because of this she somehow reminded me of a painting I had once seen of a four-masted schooner in full canvas running before the wind.

'What's his temperature today?' the doctor asked, pointing at me.

'Just over a hundred, doctor,' the Matron told him.

'He's been up here long enough,' the doctor said. 'Send him back to school tomorrow.' Then he turned to Ellis. 'Take off your pyjama trousers,' he said. He was a very small doctor, with steel-rimmed spectacles and a bald head. He frightened the life out of me.

Ellis removed his pyjama trousers. The doctor bent forward and looked at the boil. 'Hmmm,' he said. 'That's a nasty one, isn't it? We're going to have to do something about that, aren't we, Ellis?'

'What are you going to do?' Ellis asked, trembling.

'Nothing for you to worry about,' the doctor said. 'Just lie back and take no notice of me.'

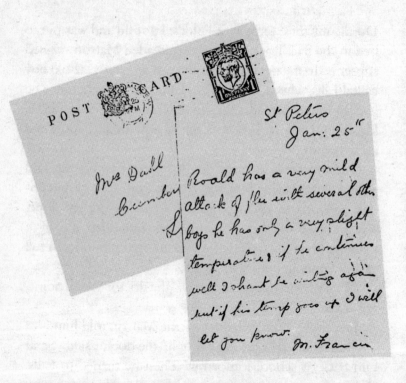

St Peters
Jan: 25th

Mrs Dahl
Cumberland

Roald has a very mild attack of flue with several other boys he has only a very slight temperature if he continues well I shant be writing again but if his temp goes up I will let you know. M. Francis

Little Ellis lay back with his head on the pillow. The doctor had put his bag on the floor at the end of Ellis's bed, and now he knelt down on the floor and opened the bag. Ellis, even when he lifted his head from the pillow, couldn't see what the doctor was doing there. He was hidden by the end of the bed. But I saw everything. I saw him take out a sort of scalpel which had a long steel handle and a small pointed blade. He crouched below the end of Ellis's bed, holding the scalpel in his right hand.

'Give me a large towel, Matron,' he said.

The Matron handed him a towel.

Still crouching low and hidden from little Ellis's view by the end of the bed, the doctor unfolded the towel and spread it over the palm of his left hand. In his right hand he held the scalpel.

Ellis was frightened and suspicious. He started raising himself up on his elbows to get a better look. 'Lie down, Ellis,' the doctor said, and even as he spoke, he bounced up from the end of the bed like a jack-in-the-box and flung the outspread towel straight into Ellis's face. Almost in the same second, he thrust his right arm forward and plunged the point of the scalpel deep into the centre of the enormous boil. He gave the blade a quick twist and then withdrew it again before the wretched boy had had time to disentangle his head from the towel.

Ellis screamed. He never saw the scalpel going in and he never saw it coming out, but he felt it all right and he screamed like a stuck pig. I can see him now struggling to get the towel off his head, and when he emerged the tears were streaming down his cheeks and his huge brown eyes were staring at the doctor with a look of utter and total outrage.

'Don't make such a fuss about nothing,' the Matron said.

'Put a dressing on it, Matron,' the doctor said, 'with

plenty of mag sulph paste.' And he marched out of the room.

I couldn't really blame the doctor. I thought he handled things rather cleverly. Pain was something we were expected to endure. Anaesthetics and pain-killing injections were not much used in those days. Dentists, in particular, never bothered with them. But I doubt very much if you would be entirely happy today if a doctor threw a towel in your face and jumped on you with a knife.

as the wart on my thum has come off beautifly, but the one on my knee has'nt even turned into a blister. You meant me to learn singing did'nt you.

When I was about nine, the ancient half-sister got engaged to be married. The man of her choice was a young English doctor and that summer he came with us to Norway.

Manly lover and ancient half-sister (in background)

Romance was floating in the air like moondust and the two lovers, for some reason we younger ones could never understand, did not seem to be very keen on us tagging along with them. They went out in the boat alone. They climbed the rocks alone. They even had breakfast alone. We resented this. As a family we had always done everything together and we didn't see why the ancient half-sister should suddenly decide to do things differently even if she had become engaged. We were inclined to blame the male lover for disrupting the calm of our family life, and it was inevitable that he would have to suffer for it sooner or later.

The male lover was a great pipe-smoker. The disgusting smelly pipe was never out of his mouth except when he was eating or swimming. We even began to wonder whether he removed it when he was kissing his betrothed. He gripped the stem of the pipe in the most manly fashion between his strong white teeth and kept it there while talking to you. This annoyed us. Surely it was more polite to take it out and speak properly.

One day, we all went in our little motor-boat to an island we had never been to before, and for once the ancient half-sister and the manly lover decided to come with us. We chose this particular island because we saw some goats on it. They were climbing about on the rocks and we thought it would be fun to go and visit them. But when we landed, we found that the goats were totally wild and we couldn't get near them. So we gave up trying to make friends with them and simply sat around on the smooth rocks in our bathing costumes, enjoying the lovely sun.

The manly lover was filling his pipe. I happened to be watching him as he very carefully packed the tobacco into the bowl from a yellow oilskin pouch. He had just finished doing this and was about to light up when the ancient half-sister called on him to come swimming. So he put down the pipe and off he went.

I stared at the pipe that was lying there on the rocks. About twelve inches away from it, I saw a little heap of dried goat's droppings, each one small and round like a pale brown berry, and at that point, an interesting idea began to sprout in my mind. I picked up the pipe and knocked all the tobacco out of it. I then took the goat's droppings and teased them with my fingers until they were nicely shredded. Very gently I poured these shredded droppings into the bowl of the pipe, packing them down with my thumb just as the manly lover always did it. When that was done, I placed a thin layer of real tobacco over the top. The entire family was watching me as I did this. Nobody said a word, but I could sense a glow of approval all round. I replaced the pipe on the rock, and all of us sat back to await the return of the victim. The whole lot of us were in this together now, even my mother. I had drawn them into the plot simply by letting them see what I was doing. It was a silent, rather dangerous family conspiracy.

Back came the manly lover, dripping wet from the sea, chest out, strong and virile, healthy and sunburnt. 'Great swim!' he announced to the world. 'Splendid water! Terrific stuff!' He towelled himself vigorously, making the muscles of his biceps ripple, then he sat down on the rocks and reached for his pipe.

Nine pairs of eyes watched him intently. Nobody giggled to give the game away. We were trembling with anticipation, and a good deal of the suspense was caused by the fact that none of us knew just what was going to happen.

The manly lover put the pipe between his strong white teeth and struck a match. He held the flame over the bowl and sucked. The tobacco ignited and glowed, and the lover's head was enveloped in clouds of blue smoke. 'Ah-h-h,' he said, blowing smoke through his nostrils. 'There's nothing like a good pipe after a bracing swim.'

Still we waited. We could hardly bear the suspense. The sister who was seven couldn't bear it at all. 'What *sort* of tobacco do you put in that thing?' she asked with superb innocence.

'Navy Cut,' the male lover answered. 'Player's Navy Cut. It's the best there is. These Norwegians use all sorts of disgusting scented tobaccos, but I wouldn't touch them.'

'I didn't know they had different tastes,' the small sister went on.

'Of course they do,' the manly lover said. 'All tobaccos are different to the discriminating pipe-smoker. Navy Cut is clean and unadulterated. It's a man's smoke.' The man seemed to go out of his way to use long words like discriminating and unadulterated. We hadn't the foggiest what they meant.

The ancient half-sister, fresh from her swim and now clothed in a towel bathrobe, came and sat herself close to her manly lover. Then the two of them started giving each other those silly little glances and soppy smiles that made us all feel sick. They were far too occupied with one another to notice the awful tension that had settled over our group. They didn't even notice that every face in the crowd was turned towards them. They had sunk once again into their lovers' world where little children did not exist.

The sea was calm, the sun was shining and it was a beautiful day.

Then all of a sudden, the manly lover let out a piercing scream and his whole body shot four feet into the air. His pipe flew out of his mouth and went clattering over the rocks, and the second scream he gave was so shrill and loud that all the seagulls on the island rose up in alarm. His features were twisted like those of a person undergoing severe torture, and his skin had turned the colour of snow. He began spluttering and choking and spewing and hawking and acting generally like a man with some serious internal injury. He was completely speechless.

We stared at him, enthralled.

The ancient half-sister, who must have thought she was about to lose her future husband for ever, was pawing at him and thumping him on the back and crying, 'Darling! Darling! What's happening to you? Where does it hurt? Get the boat! Start the engine! We must rush him to a hospital quickly!' She seemed to have forgotten that there wasn't a hospital within fifty miles.

'I've been poisoned!' spluttered the manly lover. 'It's got into my lungs! It's in my chest! My chest is on fire! My stomach's going up in flames!'

'Help me get him into the boat! Quick!' cried the ancient half-sister, gripping him under the armpits. 'Don't just sit there staring! Come and help!'

'No, no, no!' cried the now not-so-manly lover. 'Leave me alone! I need air! Give me air!' He lay back and breathed in deep draughts of splendid Norwegian ocean air, and in another minute or so, he was sitting up again and was on the way to recovery.

'What in the world came over you?' asked the ancient half-sister, clasping his hands tenderly in hers.

'I can't imagine,' he murmured. 'I simply can't imagine.' His face was as still and white as virgin snow and his hands were trembling. 'There must be a reason for it,' he added. 'There's got to be a reason.'

'I know the reason!' shouted the seven-year-old sister, screaming with laughter. 'I know what it was!'

'What was it?' snapped the ancient one. 'What have you been up to? Tell me at once!'

'It's his pipe!' shouted the small sister, still convulsed with laughter.

'What's wrong with my pipe?' said the manly lover.

'You've been smoking goat's tobacco!' cried the small sister.

It took a few moments for the full meaning of these words to dawn upon the two lovers, but when it did, and when the terrible anger began to show itself on the manly

lover's face, and when he started to rise slowly and menac-
ingly to his feet, we all sprang up and ran for our lives and
jumped off the rocks into the deep water.

Repton and Shell,
1929–36
(age 13–20)

THE PRIORY HOUSE,
REPTON,
DERBY.

Love from
Ronald

Dear Mema

Thanks awfully for the parcel and your letters. We had a great supper last night. We fried the sausages and poured hieny beans over them. then we had force & cream. Those biscuits are awfully good.

Last night we had a heavy snowfall, and there is about ... of snow on the ground. Tobogganing ...

Macdonald & I ...

Photography at Repton

On ship to Newfoundland
1933

Getting dressed for the big school

When I was twelve, my mother said to me, 'I've entered you for Marlborough and Repton. Which would you like to go to?'

Both were famous Public Schools, but that was all I knew about them. 'Repton,' I said. 'I'll go to Repton.' It was an easier word to say than Marlborough.

'Very well,' my mother said. 'You shall go to Repton.'

We were living in Kent then, in a place called Bexley. Repton was up in the Midlands, near Derby, and some 140 miles away to the north. That was of no consequence. There were plenty of trains. Nobody was taken to school by car in those days. We were put on the train.

Alfhild, me, Asta, Else and dogs. Tenby.

I was exactly thirteen in September 1929 when the time came for me to go to Repton. On the day of my departure, I had first of all to get dressed for the part. I had been to London with my mother the week before to buy the school clothes, and I remember how shocked I was when I saw the outfit I was expected to wear.

'I can't possibly go about in *those*!' I cried. 'Nobody wears things like that!'

'Are you sure you haven't made a mistake?' my mother said to the shop assistant.

'If he's going to Repton, madam, he must wear these clothes,' the assistant said firmly.

And now this amazing fancy-dress was all laid out on my bed waiting to be put on. 'Put it on,' my mother said. 'Hurry up or you'll miss the train.'

'I'll look like a complete idiot,' I said. My mother went out of the room and left me to it. With immense reluctance, I began to dress myself.

First there was a white shirt with a detachable white collar. This collar was unlike any other collar I had seen. It was as stiff as a piece of perspex. At the front, the stiff points of the collar were bent over to make a pair of wings, and the whole thing was so tall that the points of the wings, as I discovered later, rubbed against the underneath of my chin. It was known as a butterfly collar.

To attach the butterfly collar to the shirt you needed a back stud and a front stud. I had never been through this rigmarole before. I must do this properly, I told myself. So first I put the back stud into the back of the collar-band of the shirt. Then I tried to attach the back of the collar to the back stud, but the collar was so stiff I couldn't get the stud through the slit. I decided to soften it with spit. I put the edge of the collar into my mouth and sucked the starch away. It worked. The stud went through the slit and the back of the collar was now attached to the back of the shirt.

I inserted the front stud into one side of the front of the shirt and slipped the shirt over my head. With the help of a mirror, I now set about pushing the top of the front stud through the first of the two slits in the front of the collar. It wouldn't go. The slit was so small and stiff and starchy that nothing would go through it. I took the shirt off and put both the front slits of the collar into my mouth and chewed them until they were soft. The starch didn't taste of anything. I put the shirt back on again and at last I was able to get the front stud through the collar-slits.

Around the collar but underneath the butterfly wings, I tied a black tie, using an ordinary tie-knot.

Dear Mama
        Thanks for your letter.
I mean half a dozen Van Heusen
Collars. not Shirts.
            Love from
                Roald.

Then came the trousers and the braces. The trousers were black with thin pinstriped grey lines running down them. I buttoned the braces on to the trousers, six buttons in all, then I put on the trousers and adjusted the braces to the correct length by sliding two brass clips up and down.

I put on a brand new pair of black shoes and laced them up.

Now for the waistcoat. This was also black and it had twelve buttons down the front and two little waistcoat pockets on either side, one above the other. I put it on and did up the buttons, starting at the top and working down.

I was glad I didn't have to chew each of those button-holes to get the buttons through them.

All this was bad enough for a boy who had never before worn anything more elaborate than a pair of shorts and a blazer. But the jacket put the lid on it. It wasn't actually a jacket, it was a sort of tail-coat, and it was without a doubt the most ridiculous garment I had ever seen. Like the waistcoat, it was jet black and made of a heavy serge-like material. In the front it was cut away so that the two sides met only at one point, about halfway down the waistcoat. Here there was a single button and this had to be done up. From the button downwards, the lines of the coat separated and curved away behind the legs of the wearer and came together again at the backs of the knees, forming a pair of 'tails'. These tails were sepa-rated by a slit and when you walked about they flapped against your legs. I put the thing on and did up the front button. Feeling like an undertaker's apprentice in a funeral parlour, I crept downstairs.

My sisters shrieked with laughter when I appeared. 'He can't go out in *those*!' they cried. 'He'll be arrested by the police!'

the hat-band being something like this: ——————, the white stripes are realy blue, and the bit filled in is black.
P. H.

'Put your hat on,' my mother said, handing me a stiff wide-brimmed straw-hat with a blue and black band around it. I put it on and did my best to look dignified. The sisters fell all over the room laughing.

My mother got me out of the house before I lost my nerve completely and together we walked through the village to Bexley station. My mother was going to accompany me to London and see me on to the Derby train, but she had been told that on no account should she travel farther than that. I had only a small suitcase to carry. My trunk had been sent on ahead labelled 'Luggage in Advance'.

'Nobody's taking the slightest notice of you,' my mother said as we walked through Bexley High Street.

And curiously enough nobody was.

'I have learnt one thing about England,' my mother went on. 'It is a country where men love to wear uniforms and eccentric clothes. Two hundred years ago their clothes were even more eccentric then they are today. You can consider yourself lucky you don't have to wear a wig on your head and ruffles on your sleeves.'

'I still feel an ass,' I said.

'Everyone who looks at you', my mother said, 'knows that you are going away to a Public School. All English Public Schools have their own different crazy uniforms. People will be thinking how lucky you are to be going to one of those famous places.'

We took the train from Bexley to Charing Cross and then went by taxi to Euston Station. At Euston, I was put on the train for Derby with a lot of other boys who all wore the same ridiculous clothes as me, and away I went.

Beagling, Repton 1930.

Boazers

At Repton, prefects were never called prefects. They were called Boazers, and they had the power of life and death over us junior boys. They could summon us down in our pyjamas at night-time and thrash us for leaving just one football sock on the floor of the changing-room when it should have been hung up on a peg. A Boazer could thrash us for a hundred and one other piddling little misdemeanours – for burning his toast at tea-time, for failing to dust his study properly, for failing to get his study fire burning in spite of spending half your pocket money on firelighters, for being late at roll-call, for talking in evening Prep, for forgetting to change into house-shoes at six o'clock. The list was endless.

'Four with the dressing-gown on or three with it off?' the Boazer would say to you in the changing-room late at night.

Others in the dormitory had told you what to answer to this question. 'Four with it on,' you mumbled, trembling.

This Boazer was famous for the speed of his strokes. Most of them paused between each stroke to prolong the operation, but Williamson, the great footballer, cricketer and athlete, always delivered his strokes in a series of swift back and forth movements without any pause between them at all. Four strokes would rain down upon your bottom so fast that it was all over in four seconds.

A ritual took place in the dormitory after each beating. The victim was required to stand in the middle of the room and lower his pyjama trousers so that the damage could be inspected. Half a dozen experts would crowd round you and express their opinions in highly professional language.

'*What* a super job.'

'He's got *every single* one in the same place!'

'Crikey! Nobody could tell you had more than *one*, except for the mess!'

'Boy, that Williamson's got a *terrific* eye!'

'*Of course* he's got a terrific eye! Why d'you think he's a Cricket Teamer?'

'There's no wet blood though! If you had had just one more he'd have got some blood out!'

'Through a *dressing-gown*, too! It's pretty amazing, isn't it!'

'Most Boazers couldn't get a result like that *without* a dressing-gown!'

'You must have tremendously thin skin! Even Williamson couldn't have done that to *ordinary* skin!'

'Did he use the long one or the short one?'

'Hang *on*! Don't pull them up yet! I've *got* to see this again!'

And I would stand there, slightly bemused by this cool clinical approach. Once, I was still standing in the middle of the dormitory with my pyjama trousers around my knees when Williamson came through the door. 'What on earth do you think you're doing?' he said, knowing very well exactly what I was doing.

'N-nothing,' I stammered. 'N-nothing at all.'

'Pull those pyjamas up and get into bed immediately!' he ordered, but I noticed that as he turned away to go out of the door, he craned his head ever so slightly to one side to catch a glimpse of my bare bottom and his own handi-work. I was certain I detected a little glimmer of pride around the edges of his mouth before he closed the door behind him.

The Headmaster

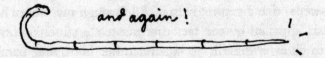

and again!

The Headmaster, while I was at Repton, struck me as being a rather shoddy bandy-legged little fellow with a big bald head and lots of energy but not much charm. Mind you, I never did know him well because in all those months and years I was at the school, I doubt whether he addressed more than six sentences to me altogether. So perhaps it was wrong of me to form a judgement like that.

What is so interesting about this Headmaster is that he became a famous person later on. At the end of my third year, he was suddenly appointed Bishop of Chester and off he went to live in a palace by the River Dee. I remember at the time trying to puzzle out how on earth a person could suddenly leap from being a schoolmaster to becoming a Bishop all in one jump, but there were bigger puzzles to come.

From Chester, he was soon promoted again to become Bishop of London, and from there, after not all that many years, he bounced up the ladder once more to get the top job of them all, Archbishop of Canterbury! And not long after that it was he himself who had the task of crowning our present Queen in Westminster Abbey with half the world watching him on television. Well, well, well! And this was the man who used to deliver the most vicious beatings to the boys under his care!

By now I am sure you will be wondering why I lay so much emphasis upon school beatings in these pages. The answer is that I cannot help it. All through my school life I was appalled by the fact that masters and senior boys were allowed literally to wound other boys, and some-times quite severely. I couldn't get over it. I never have got over it. It would, of course, be unfair to suggest that *all* masters were constantly beating the daylights out of *all* the boys in those days. They weren't. Only a few did so, but that was quite enough to leave a lasting impression of horror upon me. It left another more physical impression upon me as well. Even today, whenever I have to sit for any length of time on a hard bench or chair, I begin to feel my heart beating along the old lines that the cane made on my bottom some fifty-five years ago.

There is nothing wrong with a few quick sharp tickles on the rump. They probably do a naughty boy a lot of good. But this Headmaster we were talking about wasn't just tickling you when he took out his cane to deliver a flogging. He never flogged me, thank goodness, but I was given a vivid description of one of these ceremonies by my best friend at Repton, whose name was Michael. Michael was ordered to take down his trousers and kneel on the Headmaster's sofa with the top half of his body hanging over one end of the sofa. The great man then gave him one terrific crack. After that, there was a pause. The cane was put down and the Headmaster began filling his pipe from a tin of tobacco. He also started to lecture the kneeling boy about sin and wrongdoing. Soon, the cane was picked up again and a second tremendous crack was administered upon the trembling buttocks. Then the pipe-filling business and the lecture went on for maybe another thirty seconds. Then came the third crack of the cane. Then the instrument of torture was put once more upon the table and a box of matches was produced. A match was struck and applied to the pipe. The pipe failed to light properly. A fourth stroke was delivered, with the lecture continuing. This slow and fearsome process went on until ten terrible strokes had been delivered, and all the time, over the pipe-lighting and the match-striking, the lecture on evil and wrongdoing and sinning and misdeeds and malpractice went on without a stop. It even went on as the strokes were being administered. At the end of it all, a basin, a sponge and a small clean towel were produced by the Headmaster, and the victim was told to wash away the blood before pulling up his trousers.

Do you wonder then that this man's behaviour used to puzzle me tremendously? He was an ordinary clergyman at that time as well as being Headmaster, and I would sit in the dim light of the school chapel and listen to him preaching about the Lamb of God and about Mercy and Forgiveness and all the rest of it and my young mind would become totally confused. I knew very well that only the night before this preacher had shown neither Forgiveness nor Mercy in flogging some small boy who had broken the rules.

So what was it all about? I used to ask myself.

Did they preach one thing and practise another, these men of God?

Chocolates

Every now and again, a plain grey cardboard box was dished out to each boy in our House, and this, believe it or not, was a present from the great chocolate manufacturers, Cadbury. Inside the box there were twelve bars of chocolate, all of different shapes, all with different fillings and all with numbers from one to twelve stamped on the chocolate underneath. Eleven of these bars were new inventions from the factory. The twelfth was the 'control' bar, one that we all knew well, usually a Cadbury's Coffee Cream bar. Also in the box was a sheet of paper with the numbers one to twelve on it as well as two blank columns, one for giving marks to each chocolate from nought to ten, and the other for comments.

All we were required to do in return for this splendid gift was to taste very carefully each bar of chocolate, give it marks and make an intelligent comment on why we liked it or disliked it.

It was a clever stunt. Cadbury's were using some of the greatest chocolate-bar experts in the world to test out their new inventions. We were of a sensible age, between thirteen and eighteen, and we knew intimately every chocolate bar in existence, from the Milk Flake to the Lemon Marshmallow. Quite obviously our opinions on anything new would be valuable. All of us entered into this game with great gusto, sitting in our studies and nibbling each bar with the air of connoisseurs, giving our marks and making our comments. 'Too subtle for the common palate,' was one note that I remember writing down.

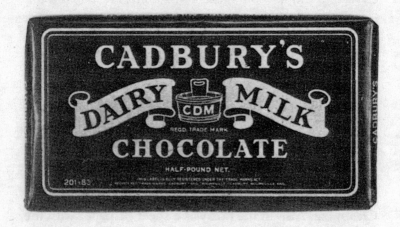

For me, the importance of all this was that I began to realize that the large chocolate companies actually did possess inventing rooms and they took their inventing very seriously. I used to picture a long white room like a laboratory with pots of chocolate and fudge and all sorts of other delicious fillings bubbling away on the stoves, while men and women in white coats moved between the bubbling pots, tasting and mixing and concocting their wonderful new inventions. I used to imagine myself working in one of these labs and suddenly I would come up with something so absolutely unbearably delicious that I would grab it in my hand and go rushing out of the lab and along the corridor and right into the office of the great Mr Cadbury himself. 'I've got it, sir!' I would shout, putting the chocolate in front of him. 'It's fantastic! It's fabulous! It's marvellous! It's irresistible!'

Slowly, the great man would pick up my newly invented chocolate and he would take a small bite. He would roll it round his mouth. Then all at once, he would leap up from his chair, crying, 'You've got it! You've done it! It's a miracle!' He would slap me on the back and shout, 'We'll sell it by the million! We'll sweep the world with this one! How on earth did you do it? Your salary is doubled!'

It was lovely dreaming those dreams, and I have no doubt at all that, thirty-five years later, when I was looking for a plot for my second book for children, I remembered those little cardboard boxes and the newly-invented chocolates inside them, and I began to write a book called *Charlie and the Chocolate Factory*.

Saturday, first I broke it in half, and only half came out, then the other bit came out, it was my dog tooth, and it was a very bad one, I am glad it came out. Will you please send me a few sweets because we had none, last week, I am sorry my writing is so untidy, but I have not much time on week days.

Corkers

There were about thirty or more masters at Repton and most of them were amazingly dull and totally colourless and completely uninterested in boys. But Corkers, an eccentric old bachelor, was neither dull nor colourless. Corkers was a charmer, a vast ungainly man with drooping bloodhound cheeks and filthy clothes. He wore creaseless flannel trousers and a brown tweed jacket with patches all over it and bits of dried food on the lapels. He was meant to teach us mathematics, but in truth he taught us nothing at all and that was the way he meant it to be. His lessons consisted of an endless series of distractions all invented by him so that the subject of mathematics would never have to be discussed. He would come lumbering into the classroom and sit down at his desk and glare at the class. We would wait expectantly, wondering what was coming next.

'Let's have a look at the crossword puzzle in today's *Times*,' he would say, fishing a crumpled newspaper out of his jacket pocket. 'That'll be a lot more fun than fiddling around with figures. I hate figures. Figures are probably the dreariest things on this earth.'

'Then why do you teach mathematics, sir?' somebody asked him.

'I don't,' he said, smiling slyly. 'I only *pretend* to teach it.'

Corkers would proceed to draw the framework of the

crossword on the blackboard and we would all spend the rest of the lesson trying to solve it while he read out the clues. We enjoyed that.

The only time I can remember him vaguely touching upon mathematics was when he whisked a square of tissue-paper out of his pocket and waved it around. 'Look at this,' he said. 'This tissue-paper is one-hundredth of an inch thick. I fold it once, making it double. I fold it again, making it four thicknesses. Now then, I will give a large bar of Cadbury's Fruit and Nut Milk Chocolate to any boy who can tell me, to the nearest twelve inches, how thick it will be if I fold it fifty times.'

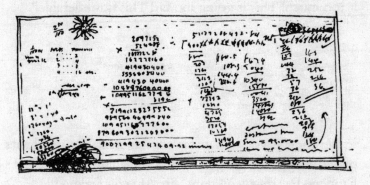

We all stuck up our hands and started guessing. 'Twenty-four inches, sir' . . . 'Three feet, sir' . . . 'Five yards, sir' . . . 'Three inches, sir.'

'You're not very clever, are you,' Corkers said. 'The answer is the distance from the earth to the sun. That's how thick it would be.' We were enthralled by this piece of intelligence and asked him to prove it on the blackboard, which he did.

Another time, he brought a two-foot-long grass-snake

into class and insisted that every boy should handle it in order to cure us for ever, as he said, of a fear of snakes. This caused quite a commotion.

I cannot remember all the other thousands of splendid things that old Corkers cooked up to keep his class happy, but there was one that I shall never forget which was repeated at intervals of about three weeks throughout each term. He would be talking to us about this or that when suddenly he would stop in mid-sentence and a look of intense pain would cloud his ancient countenance. Then his head would come up and his great nose would begin to sniff the air and he would cry aloud, 'By God! This is too much! This is going too far! This is intolerable!'

Thanks awfully for the Tablets. I took some a few times and the indigestion has stopped now, they are jolly good

We knew exactly what was coming next, but we always played along with him. 'What's the matter, sir? What's happened? Are you all right, sir? Are you feeling ill?'

Up went the great nose once again, and the head would move slowly from side to side and the nose would sniff the air delicately as though searching for a leak of gas or the smell of something burning. 'This is not to be tolerated!' he would cry. 'This is *unbearable*!'

'But what's the *matter*, sir?'

'I'll tell you what's the matter,' Corkers would shout. 'Somebody's *farted*!'

'Oh no, sir!' . . . 'Not me, sir!' . . . 'Nor me, sir!' . . . 'It's none of us, sir!'

At this point, he would rise majestically to his feet and call out at the top of his voice, *'Use door as fan! Open all windows!'*

This was the signal for frantic activity and everyone in the class would leap to his feet. It was a well-rehearsed operation and each of us knew exactly what he had to do. Four boys would man the door and begin swinging it back and forth at great speed. The rest would start clambering about on the gigantic windows which occupied one whole wall of the room, flinging the lower ones open, using a long pole with a hook on the end to open the top ones, and leaning out to gulp the fresh air in mock distress. While this was going on, Corkers himself would march serenely out of the room, muttering, 'It's the cabbage that does it! All they give you is disgusting cabbage and Brussels sprouts and you go off like fire-crackers!' And that was the last we saw of Corkers for the day.

School dinners!

Fagging

I spent two long years as a Fag at Repton, which meant I was the servant of the studyholder in whose study I had my little desk. If the studyholder happened to be a House Boazer, so much the worse for me because Boazers were a dangerous breed. During my second term, I was unfortunate enough to be put into the study of the Head of the House, a supercilious and obnoxious seventeen-year-old called Carleton. Carleton always looked at you right down

I dont think that I've told you what we do everyday sort if thing: the First bell goes at quarter-past seven, and the fag who is in water in each bedder, gets up and fills the cans with hot water, and closes the windows. Then if he wants to get into bed again. The second cell goes at half past seven, and everyone must be down for prayers by quarter to eight. Then we ...
to an how ... of m
H.

the length of his nose, and even if you were as tall as him, which I happened to be, he would tilt his head back and still manage to look at you down the length of his nose. Carleton had three Fags in his study and all of us were terrified of him, especially on Sunday mornings, because Sunday was study-cleaning time. All the Fags in all the studies had to take off their jackets, roll up their sleeves, fetch buckets and floor-cloths and get down to cleaning out their study-holder's study. And when I say cleaning out, I mean practically sterilizing the place. We scrubbed the floor and washed the windows and polished the grate and dusted the ledges and wiped the picture-frames and carefully tidied away all the hockey-sticks and cricket-bats and umbrellas.

All that Sunday morning we had been slogging away cleaning Carleton's study, and then, just before lunch Carleton himself strode into the room and said, 'You've had long enough.'

I am enclosing a time exposure of a bit of our study. You can see the gramaphone in the far corner.

'Yes, Carleton,' the three of us murmured, trembling. We stood back, breathless from our exertions, compelled as always to wait and watch the dreadful Carleton while he performed the ritual of inspection. First of all, he would go to the drawer of his desk and take out a pure-white cotton glove which he slid with much ceremony on to his right hand. Then, taking as much care and time as a surgeon in an operating theatre, he would move slowly round the study, running his white-gloved fingers along all the ledges, along the tops of the picture-frames, over the surfaces of the desks, and even over the bars of the fire-grate. Every few seconds, he would hold those white fingers up close to his face, searching for traces of dust, and we three Fags would stand there watching him, hardly daring to breathe, waiting for the dreaded moment when the great man would stop and shout, 'Ha! What's this I see?' A look of triumph would light up his face as he held up a white finger which had on it the tiniest smudge of grey dust, and he would stare at us with his slightly popping pale blue eyes and say, 'You haven't cleaned it have you? You haven't bothered to clean my study properly.'

To the three of us Fags who had been slaving away for the whole of the morning, these words were simply not true. 'We've cleaned every bit of it, Carleton,' we would answer. 'Every little bit.'

'In that case why has my finger got dust on it?' Carleton would say, tilting his head back and gazing at us down the length of his nose. 'This *is* dust, isn't it?'

We would step forward and peer at the white-gloved forefinger and at the tiny smidgin of dust that lay on it, and we would remain silent. I longed to point out to him that it was an actual impossibility to clean a much-used room to the point where no speck of dust remained, but that would have been suicide.

'Do any of you dispute the fact that this is dust?' Carleton would say, still holding up his finger. 'If I am wrong, do tell me.'

'It isn't *much* dust, Carleton.'

'I didn't ask you whether it was *much* dust or *not much* dust,' Carleton would say. 'I simply asked you whether or not it was dust. Might it, for example, be iron filings or face powder instead?'

'No, Carleton.'

'Or crushed diamonds, maybe?'

'No, Carleton.'

'Then what is it?'

'It's . . . it's dust, Carleton.'

'Thank you,' Carleton would say. 'At last you have admitted that you failed to clean my study properly. I shall therefore see all three of you in the changing-room tonight after prayers.'

You seem to have been doing a lot of painting; but when you paint the loo, dont paint the seat, leaving it wet and sticky, or some unfortunate person who has not noticed it, will adhere to it and unless his bottom is cut off, refuses he chooses to go about with the seat sticking behind him always, he will be doomed to stay where he is

The rules and rituals of fagging at Repton were so complicated that I could fill a whole book with them. A House Boazer, for example, could make any Fag in the

House do his bidding. He could stand anywhere he wanted to in the building, in the corridor, in the changing-room, in the yard, and yell 'Fa-a-ag!' at the top of his voice and every Fag in the place would have to drop what he was doing and run flat out to the source of the noise. There was always a mad stampede when the call of 'Fa-a-ag!' echoed through the House because the last boy to arrive would invariably be chosen for whatever menial or unpleasant task the Boazer had in mind.

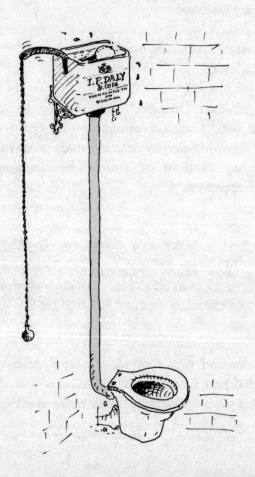

During my first term, I was in the changing-room one day just before lunch scraping the mud from the soles of my studyholder's football boots when I heard the famous shout of 'Fa-a-ag!' far away at the other end of the House. I dropped everything and ran. But I got there last, and the Boazer who had done the shouting, a massive athlete called Wilberforce, said 'Dahl, come here.'

The other Fags melted away with the speed of light and I crept forward to receive my orders. 'Go and heat my seat in the bogs,' Wilberforce said. 'I want it *warm*.'

I hadn't the faintest idea what any of this meant, but I already knew better than to ask questions of a Boazer. I hurried away and found a fellow Fag who told me the meaning of this curious order. It meant that the Boazer wished to use the lavatory but that he wanted the seat warmed for him before he sat down. The six House lavatories, none with doors, were situated in an unheated outhouse and on a cold day in winter you could get frost-bite out there if you stayed too long. This particular day was icy-cold, and I went out through the snow into the out-house and entered number one lavatory, which I knew was reserved for Boazers only. I wiped the frost off the seat with my handkerchief, then I lowered my trousers and sat down. I was there a full fifteen minutes in the freezing cold before Wilberforce arrived on the scene.

'Have you got the ice off it?' he asked.

'Yes, Wilberforce.'

'Is it *warm*?'

'It's as warm as I can get it, Wilberforce,' I said.

'We shall soon find out,' he said. 'You can get off now.'

I got off the lavatory seat and pulled up my trousers. Wilberforce lowered his own trousers and sat down. 'Very good,' he said. 'Very good indeed.' He was like a winetaster sampling an old claret. 'I shall put you on my list,' he added.

I stood there doing up my fly-buttons and not knowing what on earth he meant.

'Some Fags have cold bottoms,' he said, 'and some have hot ones. I only use hot-bottomed Fags to heat my bog-seat. I won't forget you.'

He didn't. From then on, all through that winter, I became Wilberforce's favourite bog-seat warmer, and I used always to keep a paperback book in the pocket of my tail-coat to while away the long bog-warming sessions. I must have read the entire works of Dickens sitting on that Boazer's bog during my first winter at Repton.

Games and photography

It was always a surprise to me that I was good at games. It was an even greater surprise that I was exceptionally good at two of them. One of these was called fives, the other was squash-racquets.

Fives, which many of you will know nothing about, was taken seriously at Repton and we had a dozen massive glass-roofed fives courts kept always in perfect condition. We played the game of *Eton*-fives, which is always played by four people, two on each side, and basically it consists of hitting a small, hard, white, leather-covered ball with your gloved hands. The Americans have something like it which they call handball, but Eton-fives is far more complicated because the court has all manner of ledges and buttresses built into it which help to make it a subtle and crafty game.

Fives is possibly the fastest ball-game on earth, far faster than squash, and the little ball ricochets around the court at such a speed that sometimes you can hardly see it. You need a swift eye, strong wrists and a very quick pair of hands to play fives well, and it was a game I took to right from the beginning. You may find it hard to believe, but I became so good at it that I won both the junior and the senior school fives in the same year when I was fifteen. Soon I bore the splendid title 'Captain of Fives', and

I would travel with my team to other schools like Shrewsbury and Uppingham to play matches. I loved it. It was a game without physical contact, and the quickness of the eye and the dancing of the feet were all that mattered.

A Captain of any game at Repton was an important person. He was the one who selected the members of the team for matches. He and only he could award 'colours' to others. He would award school 'colours' by walking up to the chosen boy after a match and shaking him by the hand and saying, 'Graggers on your teamer!' These were magic words. They entitled the new teamer to all manner of privileges including a different-coloured hat-band on his straw-hat and fancy braid around the edges of his blazer and different-coloured games clothes, and all sorts of other advertisements that made the teamer gloriously conspicuous among his fellows.

Fives Team
Priory House

A Captain of any game, whether it was football, cricket, fives or squash, had many other duties. It was he who pinned the notice on the school notice-board on match days announcing the team. It was he who arranged fixtures by letter with other schools. It was he and only he who had it in his power to invite this master or that to play against him and his team on certain afternoons. All these responsibilities were given to me when I became Captain of Fives. Then came the snag. It was more or less taken for granted that a Captain would be made a Boazer in recognition of his talents – if not a School Boazer then certainly a House Boazer. But the authorities did not like me. I was not to be trusted. I did not like rules. I was unpredictable. I was therefore not Boazer material. There was no way they would agree to make me a House Boazer, let alone a School Boazer. Some people are born to wield power and to exercise authority. I was not one of them. I was in full agreement with my Housemaster when he explained this to me. I would have made a rotten Boazer. I would have let down the whole principle of Boazerdom by refusing to beat the Fags. I was probably the only Captain of any game who has never become a Boazer at Repton. I was certainly the only unBoazered Double Captain, because I was also Captain of squash-racquets. And to pile glory upon glory, I was in the school football team as well.

A boy who is good at games is usually treated with great civility by the masters at an English Public School. In much the same way, the ancient Greeks revered their athletes and made statues of them in marble. Athletes were the demigods, the chosen few. They could perform glamorous feats beyond the reach of ordinary mortals. Even today, fine footballers and baseball players and runners and all other great sportsmen are much admired by the general public and advertisers use them to sell breakfast cereals. This never happened to me, and if you really want to know, I'm awfully glad it didn't.

But because I loved playing games, life for me at Repton was not totally without pleasure. Games-playing at school is always fun if you happen to be good at it, and it is hell if you are not. I was one of the lucky ones, and all those afternoons on the playing-fields and in the fives courts and in the squash courts made the otherwise grey and melancholy days pass a lot more quickly.

There was one other thing that gave me great pleasure at this school and that was photography. I was the only boy who practised it seriously, and it was not quite so simple a business fifty years ago as it is today. I made myself a little dark-room in a corner of the music building, and in there I loaded my glass plates and developed my negatives and enlarged them.

Our Arts Master was a shy retiring man called Arthur Norris who kept himself well apart from the rest of the staff. Arthur Norris and I became close friends and during my last year he organized an exhibition of my photographs. He gave the whole of the Art School over to this project and helped me to get my enlargements framed. The exhibition was rather a success, and masters who had hardly ever spoken to me over the past four years would come up and say things like, 'It's quite extraordinary' . . .

'We didn't know we had an artist in our midst' ... 'Are they for sale?'

Arthur Norris would give me tea and cakes in his flat and would talk to me about painters like Cézanne and Manet and Matisse, and I have a feeling that it was there, having tea with the gentle soft-spoken Mr Norris in his flat on Sunday afternoons that my great love of painters and their work began.

After leaving school, I continued for a long time with photography and I became quite good at it. Today, given a 35mm camera and a built-in exposure-meter, anyone can be an expert photographer, but it was not so easy fifty years ago. I used glass plates instead of film, and each of these had to be loaded into its separate container in the dark-room before I set out to take pictures. I usually carried with me six loaded plates, which allowed me only six exposures, so that clicking the shutter even once was a serious business that had to be carefully thought out beforehand.

You may not believe it, but when I was eighteen I used to win prizes and medals from the Royal Photographic Society in London, and from other places like the Photographic Society of Holland. I even got a lovely big bronze medal from the Egyptian Photographic Society in Cairo, and I still have the photograph that won it. It is a picture of one of the so-called Seven Wonders of the World, the Arch of Ctesiphon in Iraq. This is the largest unsupported arch on earth and I took the photograph while I was training out there for the RAF in 1940. I was flying over the desert solo in an old Hawker Hart biplane and I had my

camera round my neck. When I spotted the huge arch standing alone in a sea of sand, I dropped one wing and hung in my straps and let go of the stick while I took aim and clicked the shutter. It came out fine.

Goodbye school

During my last year at Repton, my mother said to me, 'Would you like to go to Oxford or Cambridge when you leave school?' In those days it was not difficult to get into either of these great universities so long as you could pay.

'No, thank you,' I said. 'I want to go straight from school to work for a company that will send me to wonderful faraway places like Africa or China.'

You must remember that there was virtually no air travel in the early 1930s. Africa was two weeks away from England by boat and it took you about five weeks to get to China. These were distant and magic lands and nobody went to them just for a holiday. You went there to work. Nowadays you can go anywhere in the world in a few hours and nothing is fabulous any more. But it was a very different matter in 1934.

So during my last term I applied for a job only to those companies that would be sure to send me abroad. They were the Shell Company (Eastern Staff), Imperial Chemicals (Eastern Staff) and a Finnish lumber company whose name I have forgotten.

I was accepted by Imperial Chemicals and by the Finnish lumber company, but for some reason I wanted most of all to get into the Shell Company. When the day came for me to go up to London for this interview, my Housemaster told me it was ridiculous for me even to try. 'The Eastern Staff of Shell are the *crème de la crème*,' he said. 'There will be at least one hundred applicants and about five vacancies. Nobody has a hope unless he's been Head of the School or Head of the House, and you aren't even a *House* Prefect!'

My Housemaster was right about the applicants. There were one hundred and seven boys waiting to be interviewed when I arrived at the Head Office of the Shell Company in London. And there were seven places to be filled. Please don't ask me how I got one of those places. I don't know myself. But get it I did, and when I told my Housemaster the good news on my return to school, he didn't congratulate me or shake me warmly by the hand. He turned away muttering, 'All I can say is I'm damned glad I don't own any shares in Shell.'

I didn't care any longer what my Housemaster thought. I was all set. I had a career. It was lovely. I was to leave school for ever in July 1934 and join the Shell Company two months later in September when I would be exactly eighteen. I was to be an Eastern Staff Trainee at a salary of five pounds a week.

That summer, for the first time in my life, I did not accompany the family to Norway. I somehow felt the need for a special kind of last fling before I became a businessman. So while still at school during my last term, I signed up to spend August with something called 'The Public Schools' Exploring Society'. The leader of this outfit was a man who had gone with Captain Scott on his last expedition to the South Pole, and he was taking a party of senior schoolboys to explore the interior of Newfoundland during the summer holidays. It sounded like fun.

Without the slightest regret I said goodbye to Repton for ever and rode back to Kent on my motorbike. This splendid machine was a 500 cc Ariel which I had bought the year before for eighteen pounds, and during my last

got the job with Shell!

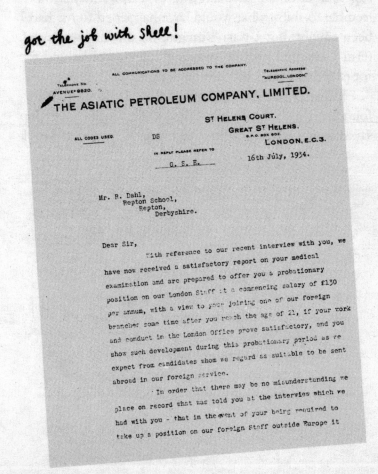

ALL COMMUNICATIONS TO BE ADDRESSED TO THE COMPANY.

TELEGRAPHIC ADDRESS "AUREDOL, LONDON."

TELEPHONE No.
AVENUE 8020.

THE ASIATIC PETROLEUM COMPANY, LIMITED.

S.ͭ HELENS COURT,
GREAT S.ͭ HELENS.
G.P.O. BOX 902.
LONDON, E.C.3.

ALL CODES USED.   DS

IN REPLY PLEASE REFER TO
G. S. E.

16th July, 1934.

Mr. R. Dahl,
   Repton School,
     Repton,
      Derbyshire.

Dear Sir,
      With reference to our recent interview with you, we have now received a satisfactory report on your medical examination and are prepared to offer you a probationary position on our London Staff at a commencing salary of £130 per annum, with a view to your joining one of our foreign branches some time after you reach the age of 21, if your work and conduct in the London Office prove satisfactory, and you show such development during this probationary period as we expect from candidates whom we regard as suitable to be sent abroad in our foreign service.

      In order that there may be no misunderstanding we place on record what was told you at the interview which we had with you - that in the event of your being required to take up a position on our foreign Staff outside Europe it term at Repton I kept it secretly in a garage along the Willington road about two miles away. On Sundays I used to walk to the garage and disguise myself in helmet, goggles, old raincoat and rubber waders and ride all over Derbyshire. It was fun to go roaring through Repton itself with nobody knowing who you were, swishing past the masters walking in the street and circling around the dangerous supercilious School Boazers out for their Sunday strolls. I tremble to think what would have happened to me had I been caught, but I wasn't caught. So on the last day of term I zoomed joyfully away and left school behind me for ever and ever. I was not quite eighteen.

I had only two days at home before I was off to Newfoundland with the Public Schools' Explorers. Our ship sailed from Liverpool at the beginning of August and took six days to reach St John's. There were about thirty boys of my own age on the expedition as well as four experienced adult leaders. But Newfoundland, as I soon found out, was not much of a country. For three weeks we trudged all over that desolate land with enormous loads on our backs. We carried tents and groundsheets and sleeping-bags and saucepans and food and axes and everything else one needs in the interior of an unmapped, uninhabitable and inhospitable country. My own load, I know, weighed exactly one hundred and fourteen pounds, and someone else always had to help me hoist the rucksack on to my back in the mornings. We lived on pemmican and lentils, and the twelve of us who went separately on what was called the Long March from the north to the south of the island and back again suffered a good deal from lack of food. I can remember very clearly how we experimented with eating boiled lichen and reindeer moss to supplement our diet. But it *was* a genuine adventure and I returned home hard and fit and ready for anything.

There followed two years of intensive training with the Shell Company in England. We were seven trainees in that year's group and each one of us was being carefully prepared to uphold the majesty of the Shell Company in one or another remote tropical country. We spent weeks at the huge Shell Haven Refinery with a special instructor who taught us all about fuel oil and diesel oil and gas oil and lubricating oil and kerosene and gasoline.

After that we spent months at the Head Office in London learning how the great company functioned from the inside. I was still living in Bexley, Kent, with my mother and three sisters, and every morning, six days a week, Saturdays included, I would dress neatly in a sombre grey suit, have breakfast at seven forty-five and then, with a brown trilby on my head and a furled umbrella in my hand, I would board the eight-fifteen train to London together with a swarm of other equally sombre-suited businessmen. I found it easy to fall into their pattern. We were all very serious and dignified gents taking the train to our offices in the City of London where each of us, so we thought, was engaged in high finance and other enormously important matters. Most of my companions wore hard bowler hats, and a few like me wore soft trilbys, but not one of us on that train in the year of 1934 went bareheaded. It wasn't done. And none of us, even on the sunniest days, went without his furled umbrella. The umbrella was our badge of office. We felt naked without it. Also it was a sign of

the Businessman

respectability. Road-menders and plumbers never went to work with umbrellas. Businessmen did.

I enjoyed it, I really did. I began to realize how simple life could be if one had a regular routine to follow with fixed hours and a fixed salary and very little original thinking to do. The life of a writer is absolute hell compared with the life of a businessman. The writer has to force himself to work. He has to make his own hours and if he doesn't go to his desk at all there is nobody to scold him. If he is a writer of fiction he lives in a world of fear. Each new day demands new ideas and he can never be sure whether he is going to come up with them or not. Two hours of writing fiction leaves this particular writer absolutely drained. For those two hours he has been miles away, he has been somewhere else, in a different place with totally different people, and the effort of swimming back into normal surroundings is very great. It is almost a shock. The writer walks out of his workroom in a daze. He wants a drink. He needs it. It happens to be a fact that nearly every writer of fiction in the world drinks more whisky than is good for him. He does it to give himself faith, hope and courage. A person is a fool to become a writer. His only compensation is absolute freedom. He has no master except his own soul, and that, I am sure, is why he does it.

The Shell Company did us proud. After twelve months at Head Office, we trainees were all sent away to various Shell branches in England to study salesmanship. I went to Somerset and spent several glorious weeks selling kerosene to old ladies in remote villages. My kerosene motor-tanker had a tap at the back and when I rolled into Shepton Mallet or Midsomer Norton or Peasedown St John or Hinton Blewett or Temple Cloud or Chew Magna or Huish Champflower, the old girls and the young maidens would hear the roar of my motor and would come out of their cottages with jugs and buckets to buy a gallon of kerosene for their lamps and their heaters. It is fun for a young man to do that sort of thing. Nobody gets a nervous breakdown or a heart attack from selling kerosene to gentle country folk from the back of a tanker in Somerset on a fine summer's day.

Then suddenly, in 1936, I was summoned back to Head Office in London. One of the Directors wished to see me. 'We are sending you to Egypt,' he said. 'It will be a three-year tour, then six months' leave. Be ready to go in one week's time.'

'Oh, but sir!' I cried out. 'Not *Egypt*! I really don't want to go to *Egypt*!'

The great man reeled back in his chair as though I had slapped him in the face with a plate of poached eggs. 'Egypt', he said slowly, 'is one of our finest and most important areas. We are doing you a *favour* in sending you there instead of to some mosquito-ridden place in the swamps!'

I kept silent.

'May I ask why you do not wish to go to Egypt?' he said.

I knew perfectly well why, but I didn't know how to put it. What I wanted was jungles and lions and elephants and tall coconut palms swaying on silvery beaches, and Egypt had none of that. Egypt was desert country. It was bare and sandy and full of tombs and relics and Egyptians and I didn't fancy it at all.

'What is wrong with Egypt?' the Director asked me again.

'It's . . . it's . . . it's', I stammered, 'it's too *dusty*, sir.'

The man stared at me. 'Too *what*?' he cried.

'Dusty,' I said.

'*Dusty*!' he shouted. 'Too *dusty*! I've never heard such rubbish!'

There was a long silence. I was expecting him to tell me to fetch my hat and coat and leave the building for ever. But he didn't do that. He was an awfully nice man and his name was Mr Godber. He gave a deep sigh and rubbed a hand over his eyes and said, 'Very well then, if that's the way you want it. Redfearn will go to Egypt instead of you and you will have to take the next posting that comes up, dusty or not. Do you understand?'

'Yes, sir, I realize that.'

'If the next vacancy happens to be Siberia,' he said, 'you'll have to take it.'

'I quite understand, sir,' I said. 'And thank you very much.'

Within a week Mr Godber summoned me again to his office. 'You're going to East Africa,' he said.

'Hooray!' I shouted, jumping up and down. 'That's marvellous, sir! That's wonderful! How terrific!'

The great man smiled. 'It's quite dusty there too,' he said.

'Lions!' I cried. 'And elephants and giraffes and coconuts everywhere!'

'Your boat leaves from London Docks in six days,' he

said. 'You get off at Mombasa. Your salary will be five hundred pounds per annum and your tour is for three years.'

I was twenty years old. I was off to East Africa where I would walk about in khaki shorts every day and wear a topi on my head! I was ecstatic. I rushed home and told my mother. 'And I'll be gone for three years,' I said.

I was her only son and we were very close. Most mothers, faced with a situation like this, would have shown a certain amount of distress. Three years is a long time and Africa was far away. There would be no visits in between. But my mother did not allow even the tiniest bit of what she must have felt to disturb my joy. 'Oh, well done *you*!' she cried. 'It's wonderful news! And it's just where you wanted to go, isn't it!'

The whole family came down to London Docks to see me off on the boat. It was a tremendous thing in those days for a young man to be going off to Africa to work. The journey alone would take two weeks, sailing through the Bay of Biscay, past Gibraltar, across the Mediterranean, through the Suez Canal and the Red Sea, calling in at Aden and arriving finally at Mombasa. What a prospect that was! I was off to the land of palm-trees and coconuts and coral reefs and lions and elephants and deadly snakes, and a white hunter who had lived ten years in Mwanza had told me that if a black mamba bit you, you died within the hour writhing in agony and foaming at the mouth. I couldn't wait.

Although I didn't know it at the time, I was sailing away for a good deal longer than three years because the Second World War was to come along in the middle of it all.

Mama, 1936

But before that happened, I got my African adventure all right. I got the roasting heat and the crocodiles and the snakes and the long safaris up-country, selling Shell oil to the men who ran the diamond mines and the sisal plantations. I learned about an extraordinary machine called a decorticator (a name I have always loved) which shredded the big leathery sisal leaves into fibre. I learned to speak Swahili and to shake the scorpions out of my mosquito boots in the mornings. I learned what it was like to get malaria and to run a temperature of 105°F for three days, and when the rainy seasons came and the water poured down in solid sheets and flooded the little dirt roads, I learned how to spend nights in the back of a stifling station-wagon with all the windows closed against marauders from the jungle. Above all, I learned how to look after myself in a way that no young person can ever do by staying in civilization.

When the big war broke out in 1939, I was in Dar es Salaam, and from there I went up to Nairobi to join the RAF. Six months later, I was a fighter pilot flying Hurricanes all round the Mediterranean. I flew in the Western Desert of Libya, in Greece, in Palestine, in Syria, in Iraq and in Egypt. I shot down some German planes and I got shot down myself, crashing in a burst of flames and crawling out and getting rescued by brave soldiers crawling on their bellies over the sand. I spent six months in hospital in Alexandria, and when I came out, I flew again.

But all that is another story. It has nothing to do with childhood or school or Gobstoppers or dead mice or Boazers or summer holidays among the islands of Norway. It is a different tale altogether, and if all goes well, I may have a shot at telling it one of these days.

Love from
BOY

Taste

First published in *The New Yorker*
(December 1951)

There were six of us to dinner that night at Mike Schofield's house in London: Mike and his wife and daughter, my wife and I, and a man called Richard Pratt.

Richard Pratt was a famous gourmet. He was president of a small society known as the Epicures, and each month he circulated privately to its members a pamphlet on food and wines. He organized dinners where sumptuous dishes and rare wines were served. He refused to smoke for fear of harming his palate, and when discussing a wine, he had a curious, rather droll habit of referring to it as though it were a living being. 'A prudent wine,' he would say, 'rather diffident and evasive, but quite prudent.' Or, 'A good-humoured wine, benevolent and cheerful – slightly obscene, perhaps, but none the less good-humoured.'

I had been to dinner at Mike's twice before when Richard Pratt was there, and on each occasion Mike and his wife had gone out of their way to produce a special meal for the famous gourmet. And this one, clearly, was to be no exception. The moment we entered the dining-room, I could see that the table was laid for a feast. The tall candles, the yellow roses, the quantity of shining silver, the three wine glasses to each person, and above all, the faint scent of roasting meat from the kitchen brought the first warm oozings of saliva to my mouth.

As we sat down, I remembered that on both Richard Pratt's previous visits Mike had played a little betting game with him over the claret, challenging him to name its breed and its vintage. Pratt had replied that that should not be difficult provided it was one of the great years. Mike had then bet him a case of the wine in question that he could not do it. Pratt had accepted, and had won both times. Tonight I felt sure that the little game would be played over again, for Mike was quite willing to lose the bet in order to prove that his wine was good enough to be recognized, and Pratt, for his part, seemed to take a grave, restrained pleasure in displaying his knowledge.

The meal began with a plate of whitebait, fried very crisp in butter, and to go with it there was a Moselle. Mike got up and poured the wine himself, and when he sat down again, I could see that he was watching Richard Pratt. He had set the bottle in front of me so that I could read the label. It said, 'Geierslay Ohligsberg, 1945'. He leaned over and whispered to me that Geierslay was a tiny village in the Moselle, almost unknown outside Germany. He said that this wine we were drinking was something unusual, that the output of the vineyard was so small that it was almost impossible for a stranger to get any of it. He had visited Geierslay personally the previous summer in order to obtain the few dozen bottles that they had finally allowed him to have.

'I doubt anyone else in the country has any of it at the

moment,' he said. I saw him glance again at Richard Pratt. 'Great thing about Moselle,' he continued, raising his voice, 'it's the perfect wine to serve before a claret. A lot of people serve a Rhine wine instead, but that's because they don't know any better. A Rhine wine will kill a delicate claret, you know that? It's barbaric to serve a Rhine before a claret. But a Moselle – ah! – a Moselle is exactly right.'

Mike Schofield was an amiable, middle-aged man. But he was a stockbroker. To be precise, he was a jobber in the stock market, and like a number of his kind, he seemed to be somewhat embarrassed, almost ashamed, to find that he had made so much money with so slight a talent. In his heart he knew that he was not really much more than a bookmaker – an unctuous, infinitely respectable, secretly unscrupulous bookmaker – and he knew that his friends knew it, too. So he was seeking now to become a man of culture, to cultivate a literary and aesthetic taste, to collect paintings, music, books and all the rest of it. His little sermon about Rhine wine and Moselle was a part of this thing, this culture that he sought.

'A charming little wine, don't you think?' he said. He was still watching Richard Pratt. I could see him give a rapid furtive glance down the table each time he dropped his head to take a mouthful of whitebait. I could almost *feel* him waiting for the moment when Pratt would take his first sip, and look up from his glass with a smile of pleasure, of astonishment, perhaps even of wonder, and then there would be a discussion and Mike would tell him about the village of Geierslay.

But Richard Pratt did not taste his wine. He was completely engrossed in conversation with Mike's eighteen-year-old daughter, Louise. He was half turned towards her, smiling at her, telling her, so far as I could gather, some story about a chef in a Paris restaurant. As he spoke, he leaned closer and closer to her, seeming in his eagerness almost to impinge upon her, and the poor girl leaned as far as she could away from him, nodding politely, rather desperately, and looking not at his face but at the topmost button of his dinner-jacket.

We finished our fish, and the maid came around removing the plates. When she came to Pratt, she saw that he had not yet touched his food, so she hesitated, and Pratt noticed her. He waved her away, broke off his conversation and quickly began to eat, popping the little crisp brown fish quickly into his mouth with rapid jabbing movements of his fork. Then, when he had finished, he reached for his glass, and in two short swallows he tipped the wine down his throat and turned immediately to resume his conversation with Louise Schofield.

Mike saw it all. I was conscious of him sitting there, very still, containing himself, looking at his guest. His round jovial face seemed to loosen slightly and to sag, but he contained himself and was still and said nothing.

Soon the maid came forward with the second course. This was a large roast of beef. She placed it on the table in front of Mike, who stood up and carved it, cutting the slices very thin, laying them gently on the plates for the maid to take around. When he had served everyone, including himself, he put down the carving knife and leaned forward with both hands on the edge of the table.

'Now,' he said, speaking to all of us but looking at Richard Pratt. 'Now for the claret. I must go and fetch the claret, if you'll excuse me.'

'You go and fetch it, Mike?' I said. 'Where is it?'

'In my study, with the cork out – breathing.'

'Why the study?'

'Acquiring room temperature, of course. It's been there twenty-four hours.'

'But why the study?'

'It's the best place in the house. Richard helped me choose it last time he was here.'

At the sound of his name, Pratt looked around.

'That's right, isn't it?' Mike said.

'Yes,' Pratt answered, nodding gravely. 'That's right.'

'On top of the green filing cabinet in my study,' Mike said. 'That's the place we chose. A good draught-free spot in a room with an even temperature. Excuse me now, will you, while I fetch it.'

The thought of another wine to play with had restored his humour, and he hurried out the door, to return a minute later more slowly, walking softly, holding in both hands a wine basket in which a dark bottle lay. The label was out of sight, facing downwards. 'Now!' he cried as he came towards the table. 'What about this one, Richard? You'll never name this one!'

Richard Pratt turned slowly and looked up at Mike; then his eyes travelled down to the bottle nestling in its small wicker basket, and he raised his eyebrows, a slight, supercilious arching of the brows, and with it a pushing outwards of the wet lower lip, suddenly imperious and ugly.

'You'll never get it,' Mike said. 'Not in a hundred years.'

'A claret?' Richard Pratt asked, condescending.

'Of course.'

'I assume, then, that it's from one of the smaller vineyards?'

'Maybe it is. Richard. And then again, maybe it isn't.'

'But it's a good year? One of the great years?'

'Yes, I guarantee that.'

'Then it shouldn't be too difficult,' Richard Pratt said, drawling his words, looking exceedingly bored. Except that, to me, there was something strange about his drawling and his boredom: between the eyes a shadow of something evil, and in his bearing an intentness that gave me a faint sense of uneasiness as I watched him.

'This one is really rather difficult,' Mike said. 'I won't force you to bet on this one.'

'Indeed. And why not?' Again the slow arching of the brows, the cool, intent look.

'Because it's difficult.'

'That's not very complimentary to me, you know.'

'My dear man,' Mike said, 'I'll bet you with pleasure, if that's what you wish.'

'It shouldn't be too hard to name it.'

'You mean you want to bet?'

'I'm perfectly willing to bet,' Richard Pratt said.

'All right, then, we'll have the usual. A case of the wine itself.'

'You don't think I'll be able to name it, do you?'

'As a matter of fact, and with all due respect, I don't,' Mike said. He was making some effort to remain polite, but Pratt was not bothering overmuch to conceal his contempt for the whole proceeding. And yet, curiously, his next question seemed to betray a certain interest.

'You like to increase the bet?'

'No, Richard. A case is plenty.'

'Would you like to bet fifty cases?'

'That would be silly.'

Mike stood very still behind his chair at the head of the table, carefully holding the bottle in its ridiculous wicker basket. There was a trace of whiteness around his nostrils now, and his mouth was shut very tight.

Pratt was lolling back in his chair, looking up at him, the eyebrows raised, the eyes half closed, a little smile touching the corners of his lips. And again I saw, or thought I saw, something distinctly disturbing about the man's face, that shadow of intentness between the eyes, and in the eyes themselves, right in their centres where it was black, a small slow spark of shrewdness, hiding.

'So you don't want to increase the bet?'

'As far as I'm concerned, old man, I don't give a damn,' Mike said. 'I'll bet you anything you like.'

The three women and I sat quietly, watching the two men. Mike's wife was becoming annoyed; her mouth had gone sour and I felt that at any moment she was going to interrupt. Our roast beef lay before us on our plates, slowly steaming.

'So you'll bet me anything I like?'

'That's what I told you. I'll bet you anything you damn well please, if you want to make an issue out of it.'

'Even ten thousand pounds?'

'Certainly I will, if that's the way you want it.' Mike was more confident now. He knew quite well that he could call any sum Pratt cared to mention.

'So you say I can name the bet?' Pratt asked again.

'That's what I said.'

There was a pause while Pratt looked slowly around the table, first at me, then at the three women, each in turn. He appeared to be reminding us that we were witness to the offer.

'Mike!' Mrs Schofield said. 'Mike, why don't we stop this nonsense and eat our food. It's getting cold.'

'But it isn't nonsense,' Pratt told her evenly. 'We're making a little bet.'

I noticed the maid standing in the background holding a dish of vegetables, wondering whether to come forward with them or not.

'All right, then,' Pratt said. 'I'll tell you what I want you to bet.'

'Come on, then,' Mike said, rather reckless. 'I don't give a damn what it is – you're on.'

Pratt nodded, and again the little smile moved the corners of his lips, and then, quite slowly, looking at Mike all the time, he said, 'I want you to bet me the hand of your daughter in marriage.'

Louise Schofield gave a jump. 'Hey!' she cried. 'No! That's not funny! Look here, Daddy, that's not funny at all.'

'No, dear,' her mother said. 'They're only joking.'

'I'm not joking,' Richard Pratt said.

'It's ridiculous,' Mike said. He was off balance again now.

'You said you'd bet anything I liked.'

'I meant money.'

'You didn't *say* money.'

'That's what I meant.'

'Then it's a pity you didn't say it. But anyway, if you wish to go back on your offer, that's quite all right with me.'

'It's not a question of going back on my offer, old man. It's a no-bet anyway, because you can't match the stake. You yourself don't happen to have a daughter to put up against mine in case you lose. And if you had, I wouldn't want to marry her.'

'I'm glad of that, dear,' his wife said.

'I'll put up anything you like,' Pratt announced. 'My house, for example. How about my house?'

'Which one?' Mike asked, joking now.

'The country one.'

'Why not the other one as well?'

'All right then, if you wish it. Both my houses.'

At that point I saw Mike pause. He took a step forward and placed the bottle in its basket gently down on the table. He moved the salt-cellar to one side, then the pepper, and then he picked up his knife, studied the blade thoughtfully for a moment, and put it down again. His daughter, too, had seen him pause.

'Now, Daddy!' she cried. 'Don't be *absurd*! It's *too* silly for words. I refuse to be betted on like this.'

'Quite right, dear,' her mother said. 'Stop it at once, Mike, and sit down and eat your food.'

Mike ignored her. He looked over at his daughter and he smiled, a slow, fatherly, protective smile. But in his eyes, suddenly, there glimmered a little triumph. 'You know,' he said, smiling as he spoke. 'You know, Louise, we ought to think about this a bit.'

'Now, stop it, Daddy! I refuse even to listen to you! Why, I've never heard anything so ridiculous in my life!'

'No, seriously, my dear. Just wait a moment and hear what I have to say.'

'But I don't *want* to hear it.'

'Louise! Please! It's like this. Richard here has offered us a serious bet. He is the one who wants to make it, not me. And if he loses, he will have to hand over a considerable amount of property. Now, wait a minute, my dear, don't interrupt. The point is this. *He cannot possibly win.*'

'He seems to think he can.'

'Now listen to me, because I know what I'm talking about. The expert, when tasting a claret – so long as it is not one of the famous great wines like Lafite or Latour – can only get a certain way towards naming the vineyard. He can, of course, tell you the Bordeaux district from which the wine comes, whether it is from St Emilion, Pomerol, Graves, or Médoc. But then each district has several communes, little counties, and each county has many, many small vineyards. It is impossible for a man to differentiate between them all by taste and smell alone. I don't mind telling you that this one I've got here is a wine from a small vineyard that is surrounded by many other small vineyards, and he'll never get it. It's impossible.'

'You can't be sure of that,' his daughter said.

'I'm telling you I can. Though I say it myself, I understand quite a bit about this wine business, you know. And anyway, heavens alive, girl, I'm your father and you don't think I'd let you in for – for something you didn't want, do you? I'm trying to make you some money.'

'Mike!' his wife said sharply. 'Stop it now, Mike, please!'

Again he ignored her. 'If you will take this bet,' he said to his daughter, 'in ten minutes you will be the owner of two large houses.'

'But I don't want two large houses, Daddy.'

'Then sell them. Sell them back to him on the spot. I'll arrange all that for you. And then, just think of it, my dear, you'll be rich! You'll be independent for the rest of your life!'

'Oh, Daddy, I don't like it. I think it's silly.'

'So do I,' the mother said. She jerked her head briskly up and down as she spoke, like a hen. 'You ought to be ashamed of yourself, Michael, ever suggesting such a thing! Your own daughter, too!'

Mike didn't even look at her. 'Take it!' he said eagerly, staring hard at the girl. 'Take it, quick! I'll guarantee you won't lose.'

'But I don't like it, Daddy.'

'Come on, girl. Take it!'

Mike was pushing her hard. He was leaning towards her, fixing her with two hard bright eyes, and it was not easy for the daughter to resist him.

'But what if I lose?'

'I keep telling you, you can't lose. I'll guarantee it.'

'Oh, Daddy, must I?'

'I'm making you a fortune. So come on now. What do you say, Louise? All right?'

For the last time, she hesitated. Then she gave a helpless little shrug of the shoulders and said, 'Oh all right then. Just so long as you swear there's no danger of losing.'

'Good!' Mike cried. 'That's fine! Then it's a bet!'

'Yes,' Richard Pratt said, looking at the girl. 'It's a bet.'

Immediately, Mike picked up the wine, tipped the first thimbleful into his own glass, then skipped excitedly around the table filling up the others. Now everyone was watching Richard Pratt, watching his face as he reached slowly for his glass with his right hand and lifted it to his nose. The man was about fifty years old and he did not have a pleasant face. Somehow, it was all mouth – mouth and lips – the full, wet lips of the professional gourmet, the lower lip hanging downwards in the centre, a pendulous, permanently open taster's lip, shaped open to receive the rim of a glass or a morsel of food. Like a keyhole, I thought, watching it; his mouth is like a large wet keyhole.

Slowly he lifted the glass to his nose. The point of the nose entered the glass and moved over the surface of the wine, delicately sniffing. He swirled the wine gently around in the glass to receive the bouquet. His concentration was intense. He had closed his eyes, and now the whole top half of his body, the head and neck and chest, seemed to become a kind of huge sensitive smelling-machine, receiving, filtering, analysing the message from the sniffing nose.

Mike, I noticed, was lounging in his chair, apparently

unconcerned, but he was watching every move. Mrs Schofield, the wife, sat prim and upright at the other end of the table, looking straight ahead, her face tight with disapproval. The daughter, Louise, had shifted her chair away a little, and sidewise, facing the gourmet, and she, like her father, was watching closely.

For at least a minute, the smelling process continued; then, without opening his eyes or moving his head, Pratt lowered the glass to his mouth and tipped in almost half the contents. He paused, his mouth full of wine, getting the first taste; then he permitted some of it to trickle down his throat and I saw his Adam's apple move as it passed by. But most of it he retained in his mouth. And now, without swallowing again, he drew in through his lips a thin breath of air which mingled with the fumes of the wine in the mouth and passed on down into his lungs. He held the breath, blew it out through his nose, and finally began to roll the wine around under the tongue, and chewed it, actually chewed it with his teeth as though it were bread.

It was a solemn, impressive performance, and I must say he did it well.

'Um,' he said, putting down the glass, running a pink tongue over his lips. 'Um – yes. A very interesting little wine – gentle and gracious, almost feminine in the after taste.'

There was an excess of saliva in his mouth, and as he spoke he spat an occasional bright speck of it on to the table.

'Now we can start to eliminate,' he said. 'You will pardon me for doing this carefully, but there is much at stake.

Normally I would perhaps take a bit of a chance, leaping forward quickly and landing right in the middle of the vineyard of my choice. But this time – I must move cautiously this time, must I not?' He looked up at Mike and he smiled, a thick-lipped, wet-lipped smile. Mike did not smile back.

'First, then, which district in Bordeaux does this wine come from? That is not too difficult to guess. It is far too light in the body to be from either St Emilion or Graves. It is obviously a Médoc. There's no doubt about *that*.

'Now – from which commune in Médoc does it come? That also, by elimination, should not be too difficult to decide. Margaux? No. It cannot be Margaux. It has not the violent bouquet of a Margaux. Pauillac? It cannot be Pauillac, either. It is too tender, too gentle and wistful for a Pauillac. The wine of Pauillac has a character that is almost imperious in its taste. And also, to me, a Pauillac contains just a little pith, a curious, dusty, pithy flavour that the grape acquires from the soil of the district. No, no. This – this is a very gentle wine, demure and bashful in the first taste, emerging shyly but quite graciously in the second. A little arch, perhaps, in the second taste, and a little naughty also, teasing the tongue with a trace, just a trace, of tannin. Then, in the after taste, delightful – consoling and feminine, with a certain blithely generous quality that one associates only with the wines of the commune of St Julien. Unmistakably this is a St Julien.'

He leaned back in his chair, held his hands up level with his chest, and placed the fingertips carefully together. He was becoming ridiculously pompous, but I thought that some of it was deliberate, simply to mock his host. I found myself waiting rather tensely for him to go on. The girl Louise was lighting a cigarette. Pratt heard the match strike and he turned on her, flaring suddenly with real anger. 'Please!' he said. 'Please don't do that! It's a disgusting habit, to smoke at table.'

She looked up at him, still holding the burning match in one hand, the big slow eyes settling on his face, resting there a moment, moving away again, slow and contemptuous. She bent her head and blew out the match, but continued to hold the unlighted cigarette in her fingers.

'I'm sorry, my dear,' Pratt said, 'but I simply cannot have smoking at table.'

She didn't look at him again.

'Now, let me see – where were we?' he said. 'Ah, yes. This wine is from Bordeaux, from the commune of St Julien, in the district of Médoc. So far, so good. But now we come to the more difficult part – the name of the vineyard itself. For in St Julien there are many vineyards, and as our host so rightly remarked earlier on, there is often not much difference between the wine of one and the wine of another. But we shall see.'

He paused again, closing his eyes. 'I am trying to establish the "growth",' he said. 'If I can do that, it will be half the battle. Now, let me see. This wine is obviously not from a first-growth vineyard – nor even a second. It is not a great wine. The quality, the – the – what do you call it? – the radiance, the power, is lacking. But a third growth – that it could be. And yet I doubt it. We know it is a good year – our host has said so – and this is probably flattering it a little bit. I must be careful. I must be very careful here.'

He picked up his glass and took another small sip.

'Yes,' he said, sucking his lips, 'I was right. It is a fourth growth. Now I am sure of it. A fourth growth from a very good year – from a great year, in fact. And that's what made it taste for a moment like a third- or even a second-growth wine. Good! That's better! Now we are closing in! What are the fourth-growth vineyards in the commune of St Julien?'

Again he paused, took up his glass, and held the rim against that sagging pendulous lower lip of his. Then I saw the tongue shoot out, pink and narrow, the tip of it dipping into the wine, withdrawing swiftly again – a repulsive sight. When he lowered the glass, his eyes remained closed, the face concentrated, only the lips moving, sliding over each other like two pieces of wet, spongy rubber.

'There it is again!' he cried. 'Tannin in the middle taste, and the quick astringent squeeze upon the tongue. Yes, yes, of course! Now I have it! This wine comes from one of those small vineyards around Beychevelle. I remember now. The Beychevelle district, and the river and the little harbour that has silted up so the wine ships can no longer use it. Beychevelle . . . could it actually be a Beychevelle itself? No, I don't think so. Not quite. But it is somewhere very close. Château Talbot? Could it be Talbot? Yes, it could. Wait one moment.'

He sipped the wine again, and out of the side of my eye I noticed Mike Schofield and how he was leaning farther and farther forward over the table, his mouth slightly open, his small eyes fixed upon Richard Pratt.

'No. I was wrong. It was not a Talbot. A Talbot comes

forward to you just a little quicker than this one; the fruit is nearer to the surface. If it is a '34, which I believe it is, then it couldn't be Talbot. Well, well. Let me think. It is not a Beychevelle and it is not a Talbot, and yet – yet it is so close to both of them, so close, that the vineyard must be almost in between. Now, which could that be?'

He hesitated, and we waited, watching his face. Everyone, even Mike's wife, was watching him now. I heard the maid put down the dish of vegetables on the sideboard behind me, gently, so as not to disturb the silence.

'Ah!' he cried. 'I have it! Yes, I think I have it!'

For the last time, he sipped the wine. Then, still holding the glass up near his mouth, he turned to Mike and he smiled, a slow, silky smile, and he said, 'You know what this is? This is the little Château Branaire-Ducru.'

Mike sat tight, not moving.

'And the year, 1934.'

We all looked at Mike, waiting for him to turn the bottle round in its basket and show the label.

'Is that your final answer?' Mike said.

'Yes, I think so.'

'Well, is it or isn't it?'

'Yes, it is.'

'What was the name again?'

'Château Branaire-Ducru. Pretty little vineyard. Lovely old château. Know it quite well. Can't think why I didn't recognize it at once.'

'Come on, Daddy,' the girl said. 'Turn it round and let's have a peek. I want my two houses.'

'Just a minute,' Mike said. 'Wait just a minute.' He was

sitting very quiet, bewildered-looking, and his face was becoming puffy and pale, as though all the force was draining slowly out of him.

'Michael!' his wife called sharply from the other end of the table. 'What's the matter?'

'Keep out of this, Margaret, will you, please?'

Richard Pratt was looking at Mike, smiling with his mouth, his eyes small and bright. Mike was not looking at anyone.

'Daddy!' the daughter cried, agonized. 'But, Daddy, you don't mean to say he's guessed it right!'

'Now, stop worrying, my dear,' Mike said. 'There's nothing to worry about.'

I think it was more to get away from his family than anything else that Mike then turned to Richard Pratt and said, 'I'll tell you what, Richard. I think you and I better slip off into the next room and have a little chat?'

'I don't want a little chat,' Pratt said. 'All I want is to see the label on that bottle.' He knew he was a winner now; he had the bearing, the quiet arrogance of a winner, and I could see that he was prepared to become thoroughly nasty if there was any trouble. 'What are you waiting for?' he said to Mike. 'Go and turn it round.'

Then this happened: the maid, the tiny, erect figure of the maid in her white and black uniform, was standing beside Richard Pratt, holding something out in her hand. 'I believe these are yours, sir,' she said.

Pratt glanced around, saw the pair of thin horn-rimmed spectacles that she held out to him, and for a moment he hesitated. 'Are they? Perhaps they are. I don't know.'

'Yes, sir, they're yours.' The maid was an elderly woman – nearer seventy than sixty – a faithful family retainer of many years' standing. She put the spectacles down on the table beside him.

Without thanking her, Pratt took them up and slipped them into his top pocket, behind the white handkerchief.

But the maid didn't go away. She remained standing beside and slightly behind Richard Pratt, and there was something so unusual in her manner and in the way she stood there, small, motionless and erect, that I for one found myself watching her with a sudden apprehension. Her old grey face had a frosty, determined look, the lips were compressed, the little chin was out and the hands were clasped together tight before her. The curious cap on her head and the flash of white down the front of her uniform made her seem like some tiny, ruffled, white-breasted bird.

'You left them in Mr Schofield's study,' she said. Her voice was unnaturally, deliberately polite. 'On top of the green filing cabinet in his study, sir, when you happened to go in there by yourself before dinner.'

It took a few moments for the full meaning of her words to penetrate, and in the silence that followed I became aware of Mike and how he was slowly drawing himself up in his chair, and the colour coming to his face, and the eyes opening wide, and the curl of the mouth, and the dangerous little patch of whiteness beginning to spread around the area of the nostrils.

'Now, Michael!' his wife said. 'Keep calm now, Michael, dear! Keep calm!'

Galloping Foxley

First published in *Town & Country*
(November 1953)

Five days a week, for thirty-six years, I have travelled on the eight-twelve train to the City. It is never unduly crowded, and it takes me right into Cannon Street Station, only an eleven and a half minute walk from the door of my office in Austin Friars.

I have always liked the process of commuting; every phase of the little journey is a pleasure to me. There is a regularity about it that is agreeable and comforting to a person of habit, and in addition, it serves as a sort of slip-way along which I am gently but firmly launched into the waters of daily business routine.

Ours is a smallish country station and only nineteen or twenty people gather there to catch the eight twelve. We are a group that rarely changes, and when occasionally a new face appears on the platform it causes a certain dis-clamatory, protestant ripple, like a new bird in a cage of canaries.

But normally, when I arrive in the morning with my usual four minutes to spare, there they all are, these good, solid, steadfast people, standing in their right places with their right umbrellas and hats and ties and faces and their newspapers under their arms, as unchanged and unchangeable through the years as the furniture in my own living-room. I like that.

I like also my corner seat by the window and reading *The Times* to the noise and motion of the train. This part of it lasts thirty-two minutes and it seems to soothe both my brain and my fretful old body like a good long massage. Believe me, there's nothing like routine and regularity for preserving one's peace of mind. I have now made this morning journey nearly ten thousand times in all, and I enjoy it more and more every day. Also (irrelevant, but interesting), I have become a sort of clock. I can tell at once if we are running two, three or four minutes late, and I never have to look up to know which station we are stopped at.

The walk at the other end from Cannon Street to my office is neither too long nor too short – a healthy little perambulation along streets crowded with fellow commuters all proceeding to their places of work on the same orderly schedule as myself. It gives me a sense of assurance to be moving among these dependable, dignified people who stick to their jobs and don't go gadding about all over the world. Their lives, like my own, are regulated nicely by the minute hand of an accurate watch, and very often our paths cross at the same times and places on the street each day.

For example, as I turn the corner into St Swithin's Lane, I invariably come head-on with a genteel middle-aged lady who wears silver pince-nez and carries a black briefcase in her hand – a first-rate accountant, I should say, or possibly an executive in the textile industry. When I cross over Threadneedle Street by the traffic lights, nine times out of ten I pass a gentleman who wears a different garden flower in his button-hole each day. He dresses in black trousers and grey spats and is clearly a punctual and meticulous person, probably a banker, or perhaps a solicitor like myself; and several times in the last twenty-five years, as we have hurried past one another across the street, our eyes have met in a fleeting glance of mutual approval and respect.

At least half the faces I pass on this little walk are now familiar to me. And good faces they are too, my kind of faces, my kind of people – sound, sedulous, businesslike folk with none of that restlessness and glittering eye about them that you see in all these so-called clever types who want to tip the world upside down with their Labour Governments and socialized medicines and all the rest of it.

So you can see that I am, in every sense of the words, a contented commuter. Or would it be more accurate to say that I *was* a contented commuter? At the time when I wrote the little autobiographical sketch you have just read – intending to circulate it among the staff of my office as an exhortation and an example – I was giving a perfectly true account of my feelings. But that was a whole week ago, and since then something rather peculiar has happened. As a matter of fact, it started to happen last Tuesday, the very morning that I was carrying the rough draft up to Town in my pocket; and this, to me, was so timely and coincidental that I can only believe it to have been the work of God. God had read my little essay and he had said to himself, 'This man Perkins is becoming over-complacent. It is high time I taught him a lesson.' I honestly believe that's what happened.

As I say, it was last Tuesday, the Tuesday after Easter, a warm yellow spring morning, and I was striding on to the platform of our small country station with *The Times* tucked under my arm and the draft of 'The Contented Commuter' in my pocket, when I immediately became aware that something was wrong. I could actually *feel* that curious little ripple of protest running along the ranks of my fellow commuters. I stopped and glanced around.

The stranger was standing plumb in the middle of the platform, feet apart and arms folded, looking for all the world as though he owned the place. He was a biggish, thickset man, and even from behind he somehow managed to convey a powerful impression of arrogance and oil. Very definitely, he was not one of us. He carried a cane instead of an umbrella, his shoes were brown instead of black, the grey hat was cocked at a ridiculous angle, and in one way and another there seemed to be an excess of silk and polish about his person. More than this I did not care to observe. I walked straight past him with my face to the sky, adding, I sincerely hope, a touch of real frost to an atmosphere that was already cool.

The train came in. And now, try if you can to imagine my horror when the new man actually followed me into *my own* compartment! Nobody has done this to me for fifteen years. My colleagues always respect my seniority. One of my special little pleasures is to have the place to myself for at least one, sometimes two or even three stations. But here, if you please, was this fellow, this stranger, straddling the seat opposite and blowing his nose and rustling the *Daily Mail* and lighting a disgusting pipe.

I lowered my *Times* and stole a glance at his face. I suppose he was about the same age as me – sixty-two or three – but he had one of those unpleasantly handsome, brown, leathery countenances that you see nowadays in advertisements for men's shirts – the lion shooter and the polo player and the Everest climber and the tropical explorer and the racing yachtsman all rolled into one; dark eyebrows, steely eyes, strong white teeth clamping the stem of a pipe. Personally, I mistrust all handsome men. The superficial pleasures of this life come too easily to them, and they seem to walk the world as though they themselves were personally responsible for their own good looks. I don't mind a *woman* being pretty. That's different. But in a man, I'm sorry, but somehow or other I find it downright offensive. Anyway, here was this one sitting right opposite me in the carriage, and I was looking at him over the top of my *Times* when suddenly he glanced up and our eyes met.

'D'you mind the pipe?' he asked, holding it up in his fingers. That was all he said. But the sound of his voice had a sudden and extraordinary effect upon me. In fact, I think I jumped. Then I sort of froze up and sat staring at him for at least a minute before I got a hold of myself and made an answer.

'This is a smoker,' I said, 'so you may do as you please.'
'I just thought I'd ask.'

There it was again, that curiously crisp, familiar voice, clipping its words and spitting them out very hard and small like a little quick-firing gun shooting out raspberry seeds. Where had I heard it before? And why did every word seem to strike upon some tiny tender spot far back in my memory? Good heavens, I thought. Pull yourself together. What sort of nonsense is this?

The stranger returned to his paper. I pretended to do the same. But by this time I was properly put out and I couldn't concentrate at all. Instead, I kept stealing glances at him over the top of the editorial page. It was really an intolerable face, vulgarly, almost lasciviously handsome, with an oily salacious sheen all over the skin. But had I or had I not seen it before sometime in my life? I began to think I had, because now, even when I looked at it I felt a peculiar kind of discomfort that I cannot quite describe – something to do with pain and with violence, perhaps even with fear.

We spoke no more during the journey, but you can well imagine that by then my whole routine had been thoroughly upset. My day was ruined; and more than one of my clerks at the office felt the sharper edge of my tongue, particularly after luncheon, when my digestion started acting up on me as well.

The next morning, there he was again standing in the middle of the platform with his cane and his pipe and his silk scarf and his nauseatingly handsome face. I walked past him and approached a certain Mr Grummitt, a stockbroker who has been commuting with me for over twenty-eight years. I can't say I've ever had an actual conversation with him before – we are rather a reserved lot on our station – but a crisis like this will usually break the ice.

'Grummitt,' I whispered. 'Who's the bounder?'

'Search me,' Grummitt said.

'Pretty unpleasant.'

'Very.'

'Not going to be a regular, I trust.'

'Oh God,' Grummitt said.

Then the train came in.

This time, to my great relief, the man got into another compartment.

But the following morning I had him with me again.

'Well,' he said, settling back in the seat directly opposite. 'It's a *topping* day.' And once again I felt that slow uneasy stirring of the memory, stronger than ever this time, closer to the surface but not yet quite within my reach.

Then came Friday, the last day of the week. I remember it had rained as I drove to the station, but it was one of those warm sparkling April showers that last only five or six minutes, and when I walked on to the platform, all the umbrellas were rolled up and the sun was shining and there were big white clouds floating in the sky. In spite of this, I felt depressed. There was no pleasure in this journey for me any longer. I knew the stranger would be there. And sure enough, he was, standing with his legs apart just as though he owned the place and this time swinging his cane casually back and forth through the air.

The cane! That did it! I stopped like I'd been shot.

'It's Foxley!' I cried under my breath. 'Galloping Foxley! And still swinging his cane!'

I stepped closer to get a better look. I tell you I've never had such a shock in all my life. It was Foxley all right. Bruce Foxley, or Galloping Foxley as we used to call him. And the last time I'd seen him, let me see – it was at school and I was no more than twelve or thirteen years old.

At that point the train came in, and heaven help me if he didn't get into my compartment once again. He put his hat and cane up on the rack, then turned and sat down and began lighting his pipe. He glanced up at me through the smoke with those rather small cold eyes and he said, '*Ripping* day, isn't it. Just like summer.'

There was no mistaking the voice now. It hadn't changed at all. Except that the things I had been used to hearing it say were different.

'All right, Perkins,' it used to say. 'All right, you nasty little boy. I am about to beat you again.'

How long ago was that? It must be nearly fifty years. Extraordinary, though, how little the features had altered. Still the same arrogant tilt of the chin, the flaring nostrils, the contemptuous staring eyes that were too small and a shade too close together for comfort; still the same habit of thrusting his face forward at you, impinging on you, pushing you into a corner, and even the hair I could remember – coarse and slightly wavy, with just a trace of oil all over it, like a well-tossed salad. He used to keep a bottle of green hair mixture on the side table in his study – when you have to dust a room you get to know and to hate all the objects in it – and this bottle had the Royal coat of arms on the label and the name of a shop in Bond Street, and under that, in small print, it said 'By

Appointment – Hairdressers To His Majesty King Edward VII'. I remember that particularly because it seemed so funny that a shop should want to boast about being hairdresser to someone who was practically bald – even a monarch.

And now I watched Foxley settle back in his seat and begin reading his paper. It was a curious sensation, sitting only a yard away from this man who fifty years before had made me so miserable that I had once contemplated suicide. He hadn't recognized *me*; there wasn't much danger of that because of my moustache. I felt fairly sure I was safe and could sit there and watch him all I wanted.

Looking back on it, there seems little doubt that I suffered very badly at the hands of Bruce Foxley my first year in school, and strangely enough, the unwitting cause of it all was my father. I was twelve and a half when I first went off to this fine old public school. That was, let me see, in 1907. My father, who wore a silk topper and morning coat, escorted me to the station, and I can remember how we were standing on the platform among piles of wooden tuck-boxes and trunks and what seemed like thousands of very large boys milling about and talking and shouting at one another, when suddenly somebody who was wanting to get by us gave my father a great push from behind and nearly knocked him off his feet.

My father, who was a small, courteous, dignified person, turned round with surprising speed and seized the culprit by the wrist.

'Don't they teach you better manners than that at this school, young man?' he said.

The boy, at least a head taller than my father, looked down at him with a cold, arrogant-laughing glare, and said nothing.

'It seems to me,' my father said, staring back at him, 'that an apology would be in order.'

But the boy just kept on looking down his nose at my father with this funny little arrogant smile at the corners of his mouth, and his chin kept coming farther and farther out.

'You strike me as being an impudent and ill-mannered boy,' my father went on. 'And I can only pray that you are an exception in your school. I would not wish for any son of mine to pick up such habits.'

At this point, the big boy inclined his head slightly in my direction, and a pair of small, cold, rather close-together eyes looked down into mine. I was not particularly frightened at the time; I knew nothing about the power of senior boys over junior boys at public schools; and I can remember that I looked straight back at him in support of my father, whom I adored and respected.

When my father started to say something more, the boy simply turned away and sauntered slowly down the platform into the crowd.

Bruce Foxley never forgot this episode; and of course the really unlucky thing about it for me was that when I arrived at school I found myself in the same 'house' as him. Even worse than that – I was in his study. He was doing his last year, and he was a prefect – a 'boazer', we called it – and as such he was officially permitted to beat any of the fags in the house. But being in his study, I automatically became his own particular, personal slave. I was his valet and cook and maid and errand-boy, and it was my duty to see that he never lifted a finger for himself unless absolutely necessary. In no society that I know of in the world is a servant imposed upon to the extent that we wretched little fags were imposed upon by the boazers at school. In frosty or snowy weather I even had to sit on the seat of the lavatory (which was in an unheated outhouse) every morning after breakfast to warm it before Foxley came along.

I could remember how he used to saunter across the room in his loose-jointed, elegant way, and if a chair were in his path he would knock it aside and I would have to run over and pick it up. He wore silk shirts and always had a silk handkerchief tucked up his sleeve, and his shoes were made by someone called Lobb (who also had a Royal crest). They were pointed shoes, and it was my duty to rub the leather with a bone for fifteen minutes each day to make it shine.

But the worst memories of all had to do with the changing-room.

I could see myself now, a small pale shrimp of a boy standing just inside the door of this huge room in my pyjamas and bedroom slippers and brown camel-hair dressing-gown. A single bright electric bulb was hanging on a flex from the ceiling, and all around the walls the black and yellow football shirts with their sweaty smell filling the room, and the voice, the clipped, pip-spitting voice, was saying, 'So which is it to be this time? Six with the dressing-gown on – or four with it off?'

I never could bring myself to answer this question. I would simply stand there staring down at the dirty floor-planks, dizzy with fear and unable to think of anything except that this other larger boy would soon start smashing away at me with his long, thin, white stick, slowly, scientifically, skilfully, legally and with apparent relish, and I would bleed. Five hours earlier, I had failed to get the fire to light in his study. I had spent my pocket money on a box of special firelighters and I had held a newspaper across the chimney opening to make a draught and I had knelt down in front of it and blown my guts out into the bottom of the grate; but the coals would not burn.

'If you're too obstinate to answer,' the voice was saying, 'then I'll have to decide for you.'

I wanted desperately to answer because I knew which one I had to choose. It's the first thing you learn when you arrive. Always keep the dressing-gown *on* and take the extra strokes. Otherwise you're almost certain to get cut. Even three with it on is better than one with it off.

'Take it off then and get into the far corner and touch your toes. I'm going to give you four.'

Slowly I would take it off and lay it on the ledge above the boot-lockers. And slowly I would walk over to the far corner, cold and naked now in my cotton pyjamas, treading softly and seeing everything around me suddenly very bright and flat and far away, like a magic-lantern picture, and very big, and very unreal, and sort of swimming through the water in my eyes.

'Go on and touch your toes. Tighter – much tighter than that.'

Then he would walk down to the far end of the changing-room and I would be watching him upside down between my legs, and he would disappear through a doorway that led down two steps into what we called 'the basin-passage'. This was a stone-floored corridor with wash-basins along one wall, and beyond it was the bathroom. When Foxley disappeared I knew he was walking down to the far end of the basin-passage. Foxley always did that. Then, in the distance, but echoing loud among the basins and the tiles, I would hear the noise of his shoes on the stone floor as he started galloping forward, and through my legs I would see him leaping up the two steps into the changing-room and come bounding towards me with his face thrust forward and the cane held high in the air. This was the moment when I shut my eyes and waited for the crack and told myself that whatever happened I must not straighten up.

Anyone who has been properly beaten will tell you that the real pain does not come until about eight or ten seconds after the stroke. The stroke itself is merely a loud crack and a sort of blunt thud against your backside, numbing you completely. (I'm told a bullet wound does the same.) But later on, oh my heavens, it feels like someone is laying a red-hot poker right across your naked buttocks and it is absolutely impossible to prevent yourself from reaching back and clutching it with your fingers.

Foxley knew all about this time lag, and the slow walk back over a distance that must altogether have been fifteen yards gave each stroke plenty of time to reach the peak of its pain before the next one was delivered.

On the fourth stroke I would invariably straighten up. I couldn't help it. It was an automatic defence reaction from a body that had had as much as it could stand.

'You flinched,' Foxley would say. 'That one doesn't count. Go on – down you get.'

The next time I would remember to grip my ankles.

Afterwards, he would watch me as I walked over – very stiff now and holding my backside – to put on my dressing-gown, but I would always try to keep turned away from him so he couldn't see my face. And when I went out, it would be, 'Hey you! Come back!'

I was in the passage then, and I would stop and turn and stand in the doorway, waiting.

'Come here. Come on, come back here. Now – haven't you forgotten something?'

All I could think of at that moment was the excruciating burning pain in my behind.

'You strike me as being an impudent and ill-mannered boy,' he would say, imitating my father's voice. 'Don't they teach you better manners than that at this school?'

'Thank . . . you,' I would stammer. 'Thank . . . you . . . for the beating.'

And then back up the dark stairs to the dormitory and it became much better then because it was all over and the pain was going and the others were clustering round and treating me with a certain rough sympathy born of having gone through the same thing themselves, many times.

'Hey Perkins, let's have a look.'

'How many d'you get?'

'Five, wasn't it? We heard them easily from here.'

'Come on, man. Let's see the marks.'

I would take down my pyjamas and stand there while this group of experts solemnly examined the damage.

'Rather far apart, aren't they? Not quite up to Foxley's usual standard.'

'Two of them are close. Actually touching. Look – these two are beauties!'

'That low one was a rotten shot.'

'Did he go right down the basin-passage to start his run?'

'You got an extra one for flinching, didn't you?'

'By golly, old Foxley's really got it in for *you*, Perkins.'

'Bleeding a bit too. Better wash it, you know.'

Then the door would open and Foxley would be there, and everyone would scatter and pretend to be doing his teeth or saying his prayers while I was left standing in the centre of the room with my pants down.

'What's going on here?' Foxley would say, taking a quick look at his own handiwork. 'You – Perkins! Put your pyjamas on properly and get into bed.'

And that was the end of a day.

Through the week, I never had a moment of time to myself. If Foxley saw me in the study taking up a novel or perhaps opening my stamp album, he would immediately find something for me to do. One of his favourites, especially when it was raining outside, was, 'Oh Perkins, I think a bunch of wild irises would look rather nice on my desk, don't you?'

Wild irises grew only around Orange Ponds. Orange Ponds was two miles down the road and half a mile across the fields. I would get up from my chair, put on my rain-coat and my straw hat, take my umbrella – my brolly – and set off on this long and lonely trek. The straw hat had to be worn at all times outdoors, but it was easily destroyed by rain; therefore the brolly was necessary to protect the hat. On the other hand, you can't keep a brolly over your head while scrambling about on a woody bank looking for irises, so to save my hat from ruin I would put it on the ground under my brolly while I searched for the flowers. In this way, I caught many colds.

But the most dreaded day was Sunday. Sunday was for cleaning the study, and how well I can remember the ter-ror of those mornings, the frantic dusting and scrubbing, and then the waiting for Foxley to come in to inspect.

'Finished?' he would ask.

'I . . . I think so.'

Then he would stroll over to the drawer of his desk and take out a single white glove, fitting it slowly on to his right hand, pushing each finger well home, and I would stand there watching and trembling as he moved around the room running his white-gloved forefinger along the picture tops, the skirting, the shelves, the window sills, the lampshades. I never took my eyes off that finger. For me it was an instrument of doom. Nearly always, it managed to discover some tiny crack that I had overlooked or perhaps hadn't even thought about; and when this happened Fox-ley would turn slowly around, smiling that dangerous little smile that wasn't a smile, holding up the white finger so that I should see for myself the thin smudge of dust that lay along the side of it.

'Well,' he would say. 'So you're a lazy little boy. Aren't you?'

No answer.

'Aren't you?'

'I thought I dusted it all.'

'Are you or are you not a nasty, lazy little boy?'

'Y-yes.'

'But your father wouldn't want you to grow up like that, would he? Your father is very particular about manners, is he not?'

No answer.

'I asked you, is your father particular about manners?'

'Perhaps – yes.'

'Therefore I will be doing him a favour if I punish you, won't I?'

'I don't know.'

'Won't I?'

'Y-yes.'

'We will meet later then, after prayers, in the changing-room.'

The rest of the day would be spent in an agony of waiting for the evening to come.

Oh my goodness, how it was all coming back to me now. Sunday was also letter-writing time.

Dear Mummy and Daddy – thank you very much for your letter. I hope you are both well. I am, except I have got a cold because I got caught in the rain but it will soon be over. Yesterday we played Shrewsbury and beat them 4–2. I watched and Foxley who you know is the head of our house scored one of our goals. Thank you very much for the cake. With love from William.

I usually went to the lavatory to write my letter, or to the boot-hole, or the bathroom – any place out of Foxley's way. But I had to watch the time. Tea was at four thirty and Foxley's toast had to be ready. Every day I had to make toast for Foxley, and on weekdays there were no fires allowed in the studies so all the fags, each making toast for his own study-holder, would have to crowd round the one small fire in the library, jockeying for position with his toasting-fork. Under these conditions, I still had to see that Foxley's toast was (1) very crisp (2) not burned at all (3) hot and ready exactly on time. To fail in any one of these requirements was a 'beatable offence'.

'Hey you! What's this?'

'It's toast.'

'Is this really your idea of toast?'

'Well . . .'

'You're too idle to make it right, aren't you?'

'I try to make it.'

'You know what they do to an idle horse, Perkins?'

'No.'

'Are you a horse?'

'No.'

'Well – anyway you're an ass – ha, ha – so I think you qualify. I'll be seeing you later.'

Oh, the agony of those days. To burn Foxley's toast was a 'beatable offence'. So was forgetting to take the mud off Foxley's football boots. So was failing to hang up

Foxley's football clothes. So was rolling up Foxley's brolly the wrong way round. So was banging the study door when Foxley was working. So was filling Foxley's bath too hot for him. So was not cleaning the buttons properly on Foxley's OTC uniform. So was making those blue metal-polish smudges on the uniform itself. So was failing to shine the *soles* of Foxley's shoes. So was leaving Foxley's study untidy at any time. In fact, so far as Foxley was concerned, I was practically a beatable offence myself.

I glanced out the window. My goodness, we were nearly there. I must have been dreaming away like this for quite a while, and I hadn't even opened my *Times*. Foxley was still leaning back in the corner seat opposite me reading his *Daily Mail*, and through a cloud of blue smoke from his pipe I could see the top half of his face over the newspaper, the small bright eyes, the corrugated forehead, the wavy, slightly oily hair.

Looking at him now, after all that time, was a peculiar and rather exciting experience. I knew he was no longer dangerous, but the old memories were still there and I didn't feel altogether comfortable in his presence. It was something like being inside the cage with a tame tiger.

What nonsense is this? I asked myself. Don't be so stupid. My heavens, if you wanted to you could go ahead and tell him exactly what you thought of him and he couldn't touch you. Hey – that was an idea!

Except that – well – after all, was it worth it? I was too old for that sort of thing now, and I wasn't sure that I really felt much anger towards him anyway.

So what should I do? I couldn't sit there staring at him like an idiot.

At that point, a little impish fancy began to take a hold of me. What I would like to do, I told myself, would be to lean across and tap him lightly on the knee and tell him who I was. Then I would watch his face. After that, I would begin talking about our schooldays together, making it just loud enough for the other people in the carriage to hear. I would remind him playfully of some of the things he used to do to me, and perhaps even describe the changing-room beatings so as to embarrass him a trifle. A bit of teasing and discomfort wouldn't do him any harm. And it would do *me* an awful lot of good.

Suddenly he glanced up and caught me staring at him. It was the second time this had happened, and I noticed a flicker of irritation in his eyes.

All right, I told myself. Here we go. But keep it pleasant and sociable and polite. It'll be much more effective that way, more embarrassing for him.

So I smiled at him and gave him a courteous little nod. Then, raising my voice, I said, 'I do hope you'll excuse me. I'd like to introduce myself.' I was leaning forward, watching him closely so as not to miss the reaction. 'My name is Perkins – William Perkins – and I was at Repton in 1907.'

The others in the carriage were sitting very still, and I could sense that they were all listening and waiting to see what would happen next.

'I'm glad to meet you,' he said, lowering the paper to his lap. 'Mine's Fortescue – Jocelyn Fortescue, Eton, 1916.'

The Landlady

First published in the *New Yorker*,
28 November 1959

Billy Weaver had travelled down from London on the slow afternoon train, with a change at Reading on the way, and by the time he got to Bath it was about nine o'clock in the evening and the moon was coming up out of a clear starry sky over the houses opposite the station entrance. But the air was deadly cold and the wind was like a flat blade of ice on his cheeks.

'Excuse me,' he said, 'but is there a fairly cheap hotel not too far away from here?'

'Try the Bell and Dragon,' the porter answered, pointing down the road. 'They might take you in. It's about a quarter of a mile along on the other side.'

Billy thanked him and picked up his suitcase and set out to walk the quarter-mile to the Bell and Dragon. He had never been to Bath before. He didn't know anyone who lived there. But Mr Greenslade at the Head Office in London had told him it was a splendid town. 'Find your own lodgings,' he had said, 'and then go along and report to the Branch Manager as soon as you've got yourself settled.'

Billy was seventeen years old. He was wearing a new navy-blue overcoat, a new brown trilby hat, and a new brown suit, and he was feeling fine. He walked briskly down the street. He was trying to do everything briskly these days. Briskness, he had decided, was *the* one common characteristic of all successful businessmen. The big shots up at Head Office were absolutely fantastically brisk all the time. They were amazing.

There were no shops on this wide street that he was walking along, only a line of tall houses on each side, all of them identical. They had porches and pillars and four or five steps going up to their front doors, and it was obvious that once upon a time they had been very swanky residences. But now, even in the darkness, he could see that the paint was peeling from the woodwork on their doors and windows, and that the handsome white façades were cracked and blotchy from neglect.

Suddenly, in a downstairs window that was brilliantly illuminated by a street-lamp not six yards away, Billy caught sight of a printed notice propped up against the glass in one of the upper panes. It said BED AND BREAK-FAST. There was a vase of yellow chrysanthemums, tall and beautiful, standing just underneath the notice.

He stopped walking. He moved a bit closer. Green curtains (some sort of velvety material) were hanging down on either side of the window. The chrysanthemums looked wonderful beside them. He went right up and peered through the glass into the room, and the first thing he saw was a bright fire burning in the hearth. On the carpet in front of the fire, a pretty little dachshund was curled up asleep with its nose tucked into its belly. The room itself, so far as he could see in the half-darkness, was filled with pleasant furniture. There was a baby-grand piano and a big sofa and several plump armchairs; and in one corner he spotted a large parrot in a cage. Animals were usually a good sign in a place like this, Billy told himself; and all in all, it looked to him as though it would be a pretty decent house to stay in. Certainly it would be more comfortable than the Bell and Dragon.

On the other hand, a pub would be more congenial than a boarding-house. There would be beer and darts in the evenings, and lots of people to talk to, and it would probably be a good bit cheaper, too. He had stayed a couple of nights in a pub once before and he had liked it. He had never stayed in any boarding-houses, and, to be perfectly honest, he was a tiny bit frightened of them. The name itself conjured up images of watery cabbage, rapacious landladies, and a powerful smell of kippers in the living-room.

After dithering about like this in the cold for two or three minutes, Billy decided that he would walk on and take a look at the Bell and Dragon before making up his mind. He turned to go.

And now a queer thing happened to him. He was in the act of stepping back and turning away from the window when all at once his eye was caught and held in the most peculiar manner by the small notice that was there. BED AND BREAKFAST, it said. BED AND BREAKFAST, BED AND BREAKFAST, BED AND BREAKFAST. Each word was like a large black eye staring at him through the glass, holding him, compelling him, forcing him to stay where he was and not to walk away from that house, and the next thing he knew, he was actually moving across from the window to the front door of the house, climbing the steps that led up to it, and reaching for the bell.

He pressed the bell. Far away in a back room he heard it ringing, and then *at once* – it must have been at once because he hadn't even had time to take his finger from the bell-button – the door swung open and a woman was standing there.

Normally you ring the bell and you have at least a half-minute's wait before the door opens. But this dame was like a jack-in-the-box. He pressed the bell – and out she popped! It made him jump.

She was about forty-five or fifty years old, and the moment she saw him, she gave him a warm welcoming smile.

'*Please* come in,' she said pleasantly. She stepped aside, holding the door wide open, and Billy found himself automatically starting forward. The compulsion or, more accurately, the desire to follow after her into that house was extraordinarily strong.

'I saw the notice in the window,' he said, holding himself back.

'Yes, I know.'

'I was wondering about a room.'

'It's *all* ready for you, my dear,' she said. She had a round pink face and very gentle blue eyes.

'I was on my way to the Bell and Dragon,' Billy told her. 'But the notice in your window just happened to catch my eye.'

'My dear boy,' she said, 'why don't you come in out of the cold?'

'How much do you charge?'

'Five and sixpence a night, including breakfast.'

It was fantastically cheap. It was less than half of what he had been willing to pay.

'If that is too much,' she added, 'then perhaps I can reduce it just a tiny bit. Do you desire an egg for breakfast? Eggs are expensive at the moment. It would be sixpence less without the egg.'

'Five and sixpence is fine,' he answered. 'I should like very much to stay here.'

'I knew you would. Do come in.'

She seemed terribly nice. She looked exactly like the mother of one's best school-friend welcoming one into the house to stay for the Christmas holidays. Billy took off his hat, and stepped over the threshold.

'Just hang it there,' she said, 'and let me help you with your coat.'

There were no other hats or coats in the hall. There were no umbrellas, no walking-sticks – nothing.

'We have it *all* to ourselves,' she said, smiling at him over her shoulder as she led the way upstairs. 'You see, it isn't very often I have the pleasure of taking a visitor into my little nest.'

The old girl is slightly dotty, Billy told himself. But at five and sixpence a night, who gives a damn about that? 'I should've thought you'd be simply swamped with applicants,' he said politely.

'Oh, I am, my dear, I am, of course I am. But the trouble is that I'm inclined to be just a teeny weeny bit choosy and particular – if you see what I mean.'

'Ah, yes.'

'But I'm always ready. Everything is always ready day and night in this house just on the off-chance that an acceptable young gentleman will come along. And it is such a pleasure, my dear, such a very great pleasure when now and again I open the door and I see someone standing there who is just *exactly* right.' She was halfway up the stairs, and she paused with one hand on the stair-rail, turning her head and smiling down at him with pale lips. 'Like you,' she added, and her blue eyes travelled slowly all the way down the length of Billy's body, to his feet, and then up again.

On the second-floor landing she said to him, 'This floor is mine.'

They climbed up another flight. 'And this one is *all* yours,' she said. 'Here's your room. I do hope you'll like it.' She took him into a small but charming front bedroom, switching on the light as she went in.

'The morning sun comes right in the window, Mr Perkins. It *is* Mr Perkins, isn't it?'

'No,' he said. 'It's Weaver.'

'Mr Weaver. How nice. I've put a water-bottle between the sheets to air them out, Mr Weaver. It's such a comfort to have a hot water-bottle in a strange bed with clean sheets, don't you agree? And you may light the gas fire at any time if you feel chilly.'

'Thank you,' Billy said. 'Thank you ever so much.' He noticed that the bedspread had been taken off the bed, and that the bedclothes had been neatly turned back on one side, all ready for someone to get in.

'I'm so glad you appeared,' she said, looking earnestly into his face. 'I was beginning to get worried.'

'That's all right,' Billy answered brightly. 'You mustn't worry about me.' He put his suitcase on the chair and started to open it.

'And what about supper, my dear? Did you manage to get anything to eat before you came here?'

'I'm not a bit hungry, thank you,' he said. 'I think I'll just go to bed as soon as possible because tomorrow I've got to get up rather early and report to the office.'

'Very well, then. I'll leave you now so that you can unpack. But before you go to bed, would you be kind enough to pop into the sitting-room on the ground floor and sign the book? Everyone has to do that because it's the law of the land, and we don't want to go breaking any laws at *this* stage in the proceedings, do we?' She gave him a little wave of the hand and went quickly out of the room and closed the door.

Now, the fact that his landlady appeared to be slightly off her rocker didn't worry Billy in the least. After all, she not only was harmless – there was no question about that – but she was also quite obviously a kind and gener-ous soul. He guessed that she had probably lost a son in the war, or something like that, and had never gotten over it.

So a few minutes later, after unpacking his suitcase and washing his hands, he trotted downstairs to the ground floor and entered the living-room. His landlady wasn't there, but the fire was glowing in the hearth, and the little dachshund was still sleeping soundly in front of it. The room was wonderfully warm and cosy. I'm a lucky fellow, he thought, rubbing his hands. This is a bit of all right.

He found the guest-book lying open on the piano, so he took out his pen and wrote down his name and address. There were only two other entries above his on the page, and, as one always does with guest-books, he started to read them. One was a Christopher Mulholland from Cardiff. The other was Gregory W. Temple from Bristol.

That's funny, he thought suddenly. Christopher Mulholland. It rings a bell.

Now where on earth had he heard that rather unusual name before?

Was it a boy at school? No. Was it one of his sister's numerous young men, perhaps, or a friend of his father's? No, no, it wasn't any of those. He glanced down again at the book.

Christopher Mulholland   *231 Cathedral Road, Cardiff*
Gregory W. Temple   *27 Sycamore Drive, Bristol*

As a matter of fact, now he came to think of it, he wasn't at all sure that the second name didn't have almost as much of a familiar ring about it as the first.

'Gregory Temple?' he said aloud, searching his memory. 'Christopher Mulholland? . . .'

'Such charming boys,' a voice behind him answered, and he turned and saw his landlady sailing into the room with a large silver tea-tray in her hands. She was holding it well out in front of her, and rather high up, as though the tray were a pair of reins on a frisky horse.

'They sound somehow familiar,' he said.

'They do? How interesting.'

'I'm almost positive I've heard those names before somewhere. Isn't that odd? Maybe it was in the newspapers. They weren't famous in any way, were they? I mean famous cricketers or footballers or something like that?'

'Famous,' she said, setting the tea-tray down on the low table in front of the sofa. 'Oh no, I don't think they were famous. But they were incredibly handsome, both of them, I can promise you that. They were tall and young and handsome, my dear, just exactly like you.'

Once more, Billy glanced down at the book. 'Look here,' he said, noticing the dates. 'This last entry is over two years old.'

'It is?'

'Yes, indeed. And Christopher Mulholland's is nearly a year before that – more than *three years* ago.'

'Dear me,' she said, shaking her head and heaving a dainty little sigh. 'I would never have thought it. How time does fly away from us all, doesn't it, Mr Wilkins?'

'It's Weaver,' Billy said. 'W-e-a-v-e-r.'

'Oh, of course it is!' she cried, sitting down on the sofa. 'How silly of me. I do apologize. In one ear and out the other, that's me, Mr Weaver.'

'You know something?' Billy said. 'Something that's really quite extraordinary about all this?'

'No, dear, I don't.'

'Well, you see, both of these names – Mulholland and Temple – I not only seem to remember each one of them separately, so to speak, but somehow or other, in some peculiar way, they both appear to be sort of connected together as well. As though they were both famous for the same sort of thing, if you see what I mean – like . . . well . . . like Dempsey and Tunney, for example, or Churchill and Roosevelt.'

'How amusing,' she said. 'But come over here now, dear, and sit down beside me on the sofa and I'll give you a nice cup of tea and a ginger biscuit before you go to bed.'

'You really shouldn't bother,' Billy said. 'I didn't mean you to do anything like that.' He stood by the piano, watching her as she fussed about with the cups and saucers. He noticed that she had small, white, quickly moving hands, and red fingernails.

'I'm almost positive it was in the newspapers I saw them,' Billy said. 'I'll think of it in a second. I'm sure I will.'

There is nothing more tantalizing than a thing like this that lingers just outside the borders of one's memory. He hated to give up.

'Now wait a minute,' he said. 'Wait just a minute. Mulholland . . . Christopher Mulholland . . . wasn't *that* the name of the Eton schoolboy who was on a walking-tour through the West Country, and then all of a sudden . . .'

'Milk?' she said. 'And sugar?'

'Yes, please. And then all of a sudden . . .'

'Eton schoolboy?' she said. 'Oh no, my dear, that can't possibly be right because *my* Mr Mulholland was certainly not an Eton schoolboy when he came to me. He was a Cambridge undergraduate. Come over here now and sit next to me and warm yourself in front of this lovely fire. Come on. Your tea's all ready for you.' She patted the empty place beside her on the sofa, and she sat there smiling at Billy and waiting for him to come over.

He crossed the room slowly, and sat down on the edge of the sofa. She placed his teacup on the table in front of him.

'*There* we are,' she said. 'How nice and cosy this is, isn't it?'

Billy started sipping his tea. She did the same. For half a minute or so, neither of them spoke. But Billy knew that she was looking at him. Her body was half turned towards him, and he could feel her eyes resting on his face, watching him over the rim of her teacup. Now and again, he caught a whiff of a peculiar smell that seemed to emanate directly from her person. It was not in the least unpleasant, and it reminded him – well, he wasn't quite sure what it reminded him of. Pickled walnuts? New leather? Or was it the corridors of a hospital?

At length, she said, 'Mr Mulholland was a great one for his tea. Never in my life have I seen anyone drink as much tea as dear, sweet Mr Mulholland.'

'I suppose he left fairly recently,' Billy said. He was still puzzling his head about the two names. He was positive now that he had seen them in the newspapers – in the headlines.

'Left?' she said, arching her brows. 'But my dear boy, he never left. He's still here. Mr Temple is also here. They're on the fourth floor, both of them together.'

Billy set his cup down slowly on the table and stared at his landlady. She smiled back at him, and then she put out one of her white hands and patted him comfortingly on the knee. 'How old are you, my dear?' she asked.

'Seventeen.'

'Seventeen!' she cried. 'Oh, it's the perfect age! Mr Mulholland was also seventeen. But I think he was a trifle shorter than you are; in fact I'm sure he was, and his teeth weren't *quite* so white. You have the most beautiful teeth, Mr Weaver, did you know that?'

'They're not as good as they look,' Billy said. 'They've got simply masses of fillings in them at the back.'

'Mr Temple, of course, was a little older,' she said, ignoring his remark. 'He was actually twenty-eight. And yet I never would have guessed it if he hadn't told me, never in my whole life. There wasn't a *blemish* on his body.'

'A what?' Billy said.

'His skin was *just* like a baby's.'

There was a pause. Billy picked up his teacup and took another sip of his tea, then he set it down again gently in its saucer. He waited for her to say something else, but she seemed to have lapsed into another of her silences. He sat there staring straight ahead of him into the far corner of the room, biting his lower lip.

'That parrot,' he said at last. 'You know something? It had me completely fooled when I first saw it through the window. I could have sworn it was alive.'

'Alas, no longer.'

'It's most terribly clever the way it's been done,' he said. 'It doesn't look in the least bit dead. Who did it?'

'I did.'

'*You* did?'

'Of course,' she said. 'And have you met my little Basil as well?' She nodded towards the dachshund curled up so

235

comfortably in front of the fire. Billy looked at it. And suddenly, he realized that this animal had all the time been just as silent and motionless as the parrot. He put out a hand and touched it gently on the top of its back. The back was hard and cold, and when he pushed the hair to one side with his fingers, he could see the skin underneath, greyish-black and dry and perfectly preserved.

'Good gracious me,' he said. 'How absolutely fascinating.' He turned away from the dog and stared with deep admiration at the little woman beside him on the sofa. 'It must be most awfully difficult to do a thing like that.'

'Not in the least,' she said. 'I stuff *all* my little pets myself when they pass away. Will you have another cup of tea?'

'No, thank you,' Billy said. The tea tasted faintly of bitter almonds, and he didn't much care for it.

'You did sign the book, didn't you?'

'Oh yes.'

'That's good. Because later on, if I happen to forget what you were called, then I could always come down here and look it up. I still do that almost every day with Mr Mulholland and Mr . . . Mr . . .'

'Temple,' Billy said. 'Gregory Temple. Exuse my asking, but haven't there been *any* other guests here except them in the last two or three years?'

Holding her teacup high in one hand, inclining her head slightly to the left, she looked up at him out of the corners of her eyes and gave him another gentle little smile.

'No, my dear,' she said. 'Only you.'

Lucky Break

How I Became a Writer

First published in *The Wonderful Story of*
Henry Sugar (1977)

A fiction writer is a person who invents stories.

But how does one start out on a job like this? How does one become a full-time professional fiction writer?

Charles Dickens found it easy. At the age of twenty-four, he simply sat down and wrote *Pickwick Papers*, which became an immediate best-seller. But Dickens was a genius, and geniuses are different from the rest of us.

In this century (it was not always so in the last one), just about every single writer who has finally become successful in the world of fiction has started out in some other job – a schoolteacher, perhaps, or a doctor or a journalist or a lawyer. (*Alice in Wonderland* was written by a mathematician, and *The Wind in the Willows* by a civil servant.) The first attempts at writing have therefore always had to be done in spare time, usually at night.

The reason for this is obvious. When you are adult, it is necessary to earn a living. To earn a living, you must get a job. You must if possible get a job that guarantees you so much money a week. But however much you may want to take up fiction writing as a career, it would be pointless to go along to a publisher and say, 'I want a job as a fiction writer.' If you did that, he would tell you to buzz off and write the book first. And even if you brought a finished book to him and he liked it well enough to publish it, he still wouldn't give you a job. He would give you an advance of perhaps five hundred pounds, which he would get back again later by deducting it from your royalties. (A royalty, by the way, is the money that a writer gets from the publisher for each copy of his book that is sold. The average royalty a writer gets is ten per cent of the price of the book itself in the book shop. Thus, for a book selling at four pounds, the writer would get forty pence. For a paperback selling at fifty pence, he would get five pence.)

It is very common for a hopeful fiction writer to spend two years of his spare time writing a book which no publisher will publish. For that he gets nothing at all except a sense of frustration.

If he is fortunate enough to have a book accepted by a publisher, the odds are that as a first novel it will in the end sell only about three thousand copies. That will earn him maybe a thousand pounds. Most novels take at least one year to write, and one thousand pounds a year is not enough to live on these days. So you can see why a budding fiction writer invariably has to start out in another job first of all. If he doesn't, he will almost certainly starve.

Here are some of the qualities you should possess or should try to acquire if you wish to become a fiction writer:

1. You should have a lively imagination.
2. You should be able to write well. By that I mean you should be able to make a scene come alive in

the reader's mind. Not everybody has this ability. It is a gift, and you either have it or you don't.

3. You must have stamina. In other words, you must be able to stick to what you are doing and never give up, for hour after hour, day after day, week after week and month after month.

4. You must be a perfectionist. That means you must never be satisfied with what you have written until you have rewritten it again and again, making it as good as you possibly can.

5. You must have strong self-discipline. You are working alone. No one is employing you. No one is around to give you the sack if you don't turn up for work, or to tick you off if you start slacking.

6. It helps a lot if you have a keen sense of humour. This is not essential when writing for grown-ups, but for children, it's vital.

7. You must have a degree of humility. The writer who thinks that his work is marvellous is heading for trouble.

Let me tell you how I myself slid in through the back door and found myself in the world of fiction.

At the age of eight, in 1924, I was sent away to boarding-school in a town called Weston-super-Mare, on the south-west coast of England. Those were days of horror, of fierce discipline, of no talking in the dormitories, no running in the corridors, no untidiness of any sort, no this or that or the other, just rules and still more rules that had to be obeyed. And the fear of the dreaded cane hung over us like the fear of death all the time.

'The headmaster wants to see you in his study.' Words of doom. They sent shivers over the skin of your stomach. But off you went, aged perhaps nine years old, down the long bleak corridors and through an archway that took you into the headmaster's private area where only horrible things happened and the smell of pipe tobacco hung in the air like incense. You stood outside the awful black door, not daring even to knock. You took deep breaths. If only your mother were here, you told yourself, she would not let this happen. She wasn't here. You were alone. You lifted a hand and knocked softly, once.

'Come in! Ah yes, it's Dahl. Well, Dahl, it's been reported to me that you were talking during prep last night.'

'Please, sir, I broke my nib and I was only asking Jenkins if he had another one to lend me.'

'I will not tolerate talking in prep. You know that very well.'

Already this giant of a man was crossing to the tall corner cupboard and reaching up to the top of it where he kept his canes.

'Boys who break rules have to be punished.'

'Sir . . . I . . . I had a bust nib . . . I . . .'

'That is no excuse. I am going to teach you that it does not pay to talk during prep.'

He took a cane down that was about three feet long with a little curved handle at one end. It was thin and white and very whippy. 'Bend over and touch your toes. Over there by the window.'

'But, sir . . .'

'Don't argue with me, boy. Do as you're told.'

I bent over. Then I waited. He always kept you waiting for about ten seconds, and that was when your knees began to shake.

'Bend lower, boy! Touch your toes!'

I stared at the toecaps of my black shoes and I told myself that any moment now this man was going to bash the cane into me so hard that the whole of my bottom would change colour. The welts were always very long, stretching right across both buttocks, blue-black with brilliant scarlet edges, and when you ran your fingers over them ever so gently afterwards, you could feel the corrugations.

Swish! . . . Crack!

Then came the pain. It was unbelievable, unbearable, excruciating. It was as though someone had laid a white-hot poker across your backside and pressed hard.

The second stroke would be coming soon and it was as much as you could do to stop putting your hands in the way to ward it off. It was the instinctive reaction. But if you did that, it would break your fingers.

Swish! . . . Crack!

The second one landed right alongside the first and the white-hot poker was pressing deeper and deeper into the skin.

Swish! . . . Crack!

The third stroke was where the pain always reached its peak. It could go no farther. There was no way it could get any worse. Any more strokes after that simply *prolonged* the agony. You tried not to cry out. Sometimes you couldn't help it. But whether you were able to remain silent or not, it was impossible to stop the tears. They poured down your cheeks in streams and dripped on to the carpet.

The important thing was never to flinch upwards or straighten up when you were hit. If you did that, you got an extra one.

Slowly, deliberately, taking plenty of time, the head-master delivered three more strokes, making six in all.

'You may go.' The voice came from a cavern miles away, and you straightened up slowly, agonizingly, and grabbed hold of your burning buttocks with both hands and held them as tight as you could and hopped out of the room on the very tips of your toes.

That cruel cane ruled our lives. We were caned for talking in the dormitory after lights out, for talking in class, for bad work, for carving our initials on the desk, for climbing over walls, for slovenly appearance, for flicking paper-clips, for forgetting to change into house-shoes in the evenings, for not hanging up our games clothes, and above all for giving the slightest offence to any master. (They weren't called teachers in those days.) In other words, we were caned for doing everything that it was natural for small boys to do.

So we watched our words. And we watched our steps. My goodness, how we watched our steps. We became incredibly alert. Wherever we went, we walked carefully, with ears pricked for danger, like wild animals stepping softly through the woods.

Apart from the masters, there was another man in the

school who frightened us considerably. This was Mr Pople. Mr Pople was a paunchy, crimson-faced individual who acted as school-porter, boiler superintendent and general handyman. His power stemmed from the fact that he could (and he most certainly did) report us to the headmaster upon the slightest provocation. Mr Pople's moment of glory came each morning at seven thirty precisely, when he would stand at the end of the long main corridor and 'ring the bell'. The bell was huge and made of brass, with a thick wooden handle, and Mr Pople would swing it back and forth at arm's length in a special way of his own, so that it went *clangetty-clang-clang, clangetty-clang-clang, clangetty-clang-clang*. At the sound of the bell, all the boys in the school, one hundred and eighty of us, would move smartly to our positions in the corridor. We lined up against the walls on both sides and stood stiffly to attention, awaiting the headmaster's inspection.

But at least ten minutes would elapse before the headmaster arrived on the scene, and during this time, Mr Pople would conduct a ceremony so extraordinary that to this day I find it hard to believe it ever took place. There were six lavatories in the school, numbered on their doors from one to six. Mr Pople, standing at the end of the long corridor, would have in the palm of his hand six small brass discs, each with a number on it, one to six. There was absolute silence as he allowed his eye to travel down the two lines of stiffly standing boys. Then he would bark out a name, 'Arkle!'

Arkle would fall out and step briskly down the corridor to where Mr Pople stood. Mr Pople would hand him a brass disc. Arkle would then march away towards the lavatories, and to reach them he would have to walk the entire length of the corridor, past all the stationary boys, and then turn left. As soon as he was out of sight, he was allowed to look at his disc and see which lavatory number he had been given.

'Highton!' barked Mr Pople, and now Highton would fall out to receive his disc and march away.

'Angell!' . . .

'Williamson!' . . .

'Gaunt!' . . .

'Price!' . . .

In this manner, six boys selected at Mr Pople's whim were dispatched to the lavatories to do their duty. Nobody asked them if they might or might not be ready to move their bowels at seven thirty in the morning before breakfast. They were simply ordered to do so. But we considered it a great privilege to be chosen because it meant that during the headmaster's inspection we would be sitting safely out of reach in blessed privacy.

In due course, the headmaster would emerge from his private quarters and take over from Mr Pople. He walked slowly down one side of the corridor, inspecting each boy with the utmost care, strapping his wristwatch on to his wrist as he went along. The morning inspection was an unnerving experience. Every one of us was terrified of the two sharp brown eyes under their bushy eyebrows as they travelled slowly up and down the length of one's body.

'Go away and brush your hair properly. And don't let it happen again or you'll be sorry.'

'Let me see your hands. You have ink on them. Why didn't you wash it off last night?'

'Your tie is crooked, boy. Fall out and tie it again. And do it properly this time.'

'I can see mud on that shoe. Didn't I have to talk to you about that last week? Come and see me in my study after breakfast.'

And so it went on, the ghastly early-morning inspection. And by the end of it all, when the headmaster had gone away and Mr Pople started marching us into the dining-room by forms, many of us had lost our appetites for the lumpy porridge that was to come.

I have still got all my school reports from those days more than fifty years ago, and I've gone through them one by one, trying to discover a hint of promise for a future fiction writer. The subject to look at was obviously English Composition. But all my prep-school reports under this heading were flat and non-committal, excepting one. The one that took my eye was dated Christmas Term, 1928. I was then twelve, and my English teacher was Mr Victor Corrado. I remember him vividly, a tall, handsome athlete with black wavy hair and a Roman nose (who one night later on eloped with the matron, Miss Davis, and we never saw either of them again). Anyway, it so happened that Mr Corrado took us in boxing as well as in English Composition, and in this particular report it said under English, 'See his report on boxing. Precisely the same remarks apply.' So we look under Boxing, and there it says, 'Too slow and ponderous. His punches are not well timed and are easily seen coming.'

But just once a week at this school, every Saturday morning, every beautiful and blessed Saturday morning, all the shivering horrors would disappear and for two glorious hours I would experience something that came very close to ecstasy.

Unfortunately, this did not happen until one was ten years old. But no matter. Let me try to tell you what it was.

At exactly ten thirty on Saturday mornings, Mr Pople's infernal bell would go *clangetty-clang-clang*. This was a signal for the following to take place:

First, all boys of nine and under (about seventy all told) would proceed at once to the large outdoor asphalt playground behind the main building. Standing on the playground with legs apart and arms folded across her mountainous bosom was Miss Davis, the matron. If it was raining, the boys were expected to arrive in raincoats. If snowing or blowing a blizzard, then it was coats and scarves. And school caps, of course – grey with a red badge on the front – had always to be worn. But no Act of God, neither tornado nor hurricane nor volcanic eruption was ever allowed to stop those ghastly two-hour Saturday morning walks that the seven-, eight- and nine-year-old little boys had to take along the windy esplanades of Weston-super-Mare on Saturday mornings. They walked in crocodile formation, two by two, with Miss Davis striding alongside in tweed skirt and woollen stockings and a felt hat that must surely have been nibbled by rats.

The other thing that happened when Mr Pople's bell rang out on Saturday mornings was that the rest of the boys, all those of ten and over (about one hundred all told) would go immediately to the main Assembly Hall and sit down. A junior master called S. K. Jopp would then poke his head around the door and shout at us with such ferocity that specks of spit would fly from his mouth like bullets and splash against the window panes across the room. 'All right!' he shouted. 'No talking! No moving! Eyes front and hands on desks!' Then out he would pop again.

We sat still and waited. We were waiting for the lovely time we knew would be coming soon. Outside in the driveway we heard the motor-cars being started up. All were ancient. All had to be cranked by hand. (The year, don't forget, was around 1927/28.) This was a Saturday morning ritual. There were five cars in all, and into them would pile the entire staff of fourteen masters, including not only the headmaster himself but also the purple-faced Mr Pople. Then off they would roar in a cloud of blue smoke and come to rest outside a pub called, if I remember rightly, 'The Bewhiskered Earl'. There they would remain until just before lunch, drinking pint after pint of strong brown ale. And two and a half hours later, at one o'clock, we would watch them coming back, walking very carefully into the dining-room for lunch, holding on to things as they went.

So much for the masters. But what of us, the great mass of ten-, eleven- and twelve-year-olds left sitting in the Assembly Hall in a school that was suddenly without a single adult in the entire place? We knew, of course, exactly what was going to happen next. Within a minute of the departure of the masters, we would hear the front door opening, and footsteps outside, and then, with a flurry of loose clothes and jangling bracelets and flying hair, a woman would burst into the room shouting, 'Hello, everybody! Cheer up! This isn't a burial service!' or words to that effect. And this was Mrs O'Connor.

Blessed beautiful Mrs O'Connor with her whacky clothes and her grey hair flying in all directions. She was about fifty years old, with a horsey face and long yellow teeth, but to us she was beautiful. She was not on the staff. She was hired from somewhere in the town to come up on Saturday mornings and be a sort of baby-sitter, to keep us quiet for two and a half hours while the masters went off boozing at the pub.

But Mrs O'Connor was no baby-sitter. She was nothing less than a great and gifted teacher, a scholar and a lover of English Literature. Each of us was with her every Saturday morning for three years (from the age of ten until we left the school) and during that time we spanned the entire history of English Literature from AD 597 to the early nineteenth century.

Newcomers to the class were given for keeps a slim blue book called simply *The Chronological Table*, and it contained only six pages. Those six pages were filled with a very long list in chronological order of all the great and not so great landmarks in English Literature, together with their dates. Exactly one hundred of these were chosen by Mrs O'Connor and we marked them in our books and learned them by heart. Here are a few that I still remember:

AD 597	St Augustine lands in Thanet and brings Christianity to Britain
731	Bede's *Ecclesiastical History*
1215	Signing of the Magna Carta
1399	Langland's *Vision of Piers Plowman*
1476	Caxton sets up first printing press at Westminster
1478	Chaucer's *Canterbury Tales*
1485	Malory's *Morte d'Arthur*
1590	Spenser's *Faërie Queene*
1623	First Folio of Shakespeare
1667	Milton's *Paradise Lost*
1668	Dryden's *Essays*
1678	Bunyan's *Pilgrim's Progress*
1711	Addison's *Spectator*
1719	Defoe's *Robinson Crusoe*
1726	Swift's *Gulliver's Travels*
1733	Pope's *Essay on Man*
1755	Johnson's *Dictionary*
1791	Boswell's *Life of Johnson*
1833	Carlyle's *Sartor Resartus*
1859	Darwin's *Origin of Species*

Mrs O'Connor would then take each item in turn and spend one entire Saturday morning of two and a half hours talking to us about it. Thus, at the end of three years, with approximately thirty-six Saturdays in each school year, she would have covered the one hundred items.

And what marvellous exciting fun it was! She had the

great teacher's knack of making everything she spoke about come alive to us in that room. In two and a half hours, we grew to love Langland and his Piers Plowman. The next Saturday, it was Chaucer, and we loved him, too. Even rather difficult fellows like Milton and Dryden and Pope all became thrilling when Mrs O'Connor told us about their lives and read parts of their work to us aloud. And the result of all this, for me at any rate, was that by the age of thirteen I had become intensely aware of the vast heritage of literature that had been built up in England over the centuries. I also became an avid and insatiable reader of good writing.

Dear lovely Mrs O'Connor! Perhaps it was worth going to that awful school simply to experience the joy of her Saturday mornings.

At thirteen I left prep school and was sent, again as a boarder, to one of our famous British public schools. They are not, of course, public at all. They are extremely private and expensive. Mine was called Repton, in Derbyshire, and our headmaster at the time was the Reverend Geoffrey Fisher, who later became Bishop of Chester, then Bishop of London, and finally Archbishop of Canterbury. In his last job, he crowned Queen Elizabeth II in Westminster Abbey.

The clothes we had to wear at this school made us look like assistants in a funeral parlour. The jacket was black, with a cutaway front and long tails hanging down behind that came below the backs of the knees. The trousers were black with thin grey stripes. The shoes were black. There was a black waistcoat with eleven buttons to do up every morning. The tie was black. Then there was a stiff starched white butterfly collar and a white shirt.

To top it all off, the final ludicrous touch was a straw hat that had to be worn at all times out of doors except when playing games. And because the hats got soggy in the rain, we carried umbrellas for bad weather.

You can imagine what I felt like in this fancy dress when my mother took me, at the age of thirteen, to the train in London at the beginning of my first term. She kissed me good-bye and off I went.

I naturally hoped that my long-suffering backside would be given a rest at my new and more adult school, but it was not to be. The beatings at Repton were more fierce and more frequent than anything I had yet experienced. And do not think for one moment that the future Archbishop of Canterbury objected to these squalid exercises. He rolled up his sleeves and joined in with gusto. His were the bad ones, the really terrifying occasions. Some of the beatings administered by this Man of God, this future Head of the Church of England, were very brutal. To my certain knowledge he once had to produce a basin of water, a sponge and a towel so that the victim could wash the blood away afterwards.

No joke, that.

Shades of the Spanish Inquisition.

But nastiest of all, I think, was the fact that prefects were allowed to beat their fellow pupils. This was a daily occurrence. The big boys (aged 17 or 18) would flog the smaller boys (aged 13, 14, 15) in a sadistic ceremony that took place at night after you had gone up to the dormitory and got into your pyjamas.

'You're wanted down in the changing-room.'

With heavy hands, you would put on your dressing-gown and slippers. Then you would stumble downstairs and enter the large wooden-floored room where the games clothes were hanging up around the walls. A single bare electric bulb hung from the ceiling. A prefect, pompous but very dangerous, was waiting for you in the centre of the room. In his hands, he held a long cane, and he was usually flexing it back and forth as you came in.

'I suppose you know why you're here,' he would say.

'Well, I . . .'

'For the second day running you have burned my toast!'

Let me explain this ludicrous remark. You were this particular prefect's fag. That meant you were his servant, and one of your many duties was to make toast for him every day at teatime. For this, you used a long three-pronged toasting-fork, and you stuck the bread on the end of it and held it up before an open fire, first one side, then the other. But the only fire where toasting was allowed was in the library, and as teatime approached, there were never less than a dozen wretched fags all jostling for position in front of the tiny grate. I was no good at this. I usually held the bread too close and the toast got burned. But as we were never allowed to ask for a second slice and start again, the only thing to do was to scrape the burned bits off with a knife. You seldom got away with this. The prefects were expert at detecting scraped toast.

You would see your own tormentor sitting up there at the top table, picking up his toast, turning it over, examining it closely as though it were a small and very valuable painting. Then he would frown and you knew you were for it.

So now it was night-time and you were down in the changing-room in your dressing-gown and pyjamas, and the one whose toast you had burned was telling you about your crime.

'I don't like burned toast.'

'I held it too close. I'm sorry.'

'Which do you want? Four with the dressing-gown on, or three with it off?'

'Four with it on,' I said.

It was traditional to ask this question. The victim was always given a choice. But my own dressing-gown was made of thick brown camel-hair, and there was never any question in my mind that this was the better choice. To be beaten in pyjamas only was a very painful experience, and your skin nearly always got broken. But my dressing-gown stopped that from happening. The prefect knew, of course, all about this, and therefore whenever you chose to take an extra stroke and kept the dressing-gown on, he beat you with every ounce of his strength. Sometimes he would take a little run, three or four neat steps on his toes, to gain momentum and thrust, but either way, it was a savage business.

In the old days, when a man was about to be hanged, a silence would fall upon the whole prison and the other prisoners would sit very quietly in their cells until the deed had been done. Much the same thing happened at school when a beating was taking place. Upstairs in the dormitories, the boys would sit in silence on their beds in sympathy for the victim, and through the silence, from down below in the changing-room, would come the *crack* of each stroke as it was delivered.

My end-of-term reports from this school are of some interest. Here are just four of them, copied out word for word from the original documents:

Summer Term, 1930 (aged *14*). *English Composition.* 'I have never met a boy who so persistently writes the exact opposite of what he means. He seems incapable of marshalling his thoughts on paper.'

Easter Term, 1931 (aged 15). *English Composition.* 'A persistent muddler. Vocabulary negligible, sentences malconstructed. He reminds me of a camel.'

Summer Term, 1932 (aged 16). *English Composition.* 'This boy is an indolent and illiterate member of the class.'

Autumn Term, 1932 (aged 17). *English Composition.* 'Consistently idle. Ideas limited.' (And underneath this one, the future Archbishop of Canterbury had written in red ink, 'He must correct the blemishes on this sheet.')

Little wonder that it never entered my head to become a writer in those days.

When I left school at the age of eighteen, in 1934, I turned down my mother's offer (my father died when I was three) to go to university. Unless one was going to become a doctor, a lawyer, a scientist, an engineer or some other kind of professional person, I saw little point in wasting three or four years at Oxford or Cambridge, and I still hold this view. Instead, I had a passionate wish to go abroad, to travel, to see distant lands. There were almost no commercial aeroplanes in those days, and a journey to Africa or the Far East took several weeks.

So I got a job with what was called the Eastern Staff of the Shell Oil Company, where they promised me that after two or three years' training in England, I would be sent off to a foreign country.

'Which one?' I asked.

'Who knows?' the man answered. 'It depends where there is a vacancy when you reach the top of the list. It could be Egypt or China or India or almost anywhere in the world.'

That sounded like fun. It was. When my turn came to be posted abroad three years later, I was told it would be East Africa. Tropical suits were ordered and my mother helped me pack my trunk. My tour of duty was for three years in Africa, then I would be allowed home on leave for six months. I was now twenty-one years old and setting out for faraway places. I felt great. I boarded the ship at London Docks and off she sailed.

That journey took two and a half weeks. We went through the Bay of Biscay and called in at Gibraltar. We headed down the Mediterranean by way of Malta, Naples and Port Said. We went through the Suez Canal and down the Red Sea, stopping at Port Sudan, then Aden. It was tremendously exciting. For the first time, I saw great sandy deserts, and Arab soldiers mounted on camels, and palm trees with dates growing on them, and flying fish and thousands of other marvellous things. Finally we reached Mombasa, in Kenya.

At Mombasa, a man from the Shell Company came on board and told me I must transfer to a small coastal vessel and go on to Dar-es-Salaam, the capital of Tanganyika (now Tanzania). And so to Dar-es-Salaam I went, stopping at Zanzibar on the way.

For the next two years, I worked for Shell in Tanzania, with my headquarters in Dar-es-Salaam. It was a fantastic life. The heat was intense but who cared? Our dress was khaki shorts, an open shirt and a topee on the head. I learned to speak Swahili. I drove up-country visiting diamond mines, sisal plantations, gold mines and all the rest of it.

There were giraffes, elephants, zebras, lions and antelopes all over the place, and snakes as well, including the Black Mamba, which is the only snake in the world that will chase after you if it sees you. And if it catches you and bites you, you had better start saying your prayers. I learned to shake my mosquito boots upside down before putting them on in case there was a scorpion inside, and like everyone else, I got malaria and lay for three days with a temperature of one hundred and five point five.

In September 1939, it became obvious that there was going to be a war with Hitler's Germany. Tanganyika, which only twenty years before had been called German East Africa, was still full of Germans. They were everywhere. They owned shops and mines and plantations all over the country. The moment war broke out, they would have to be rounded up. But we had no army to speak of in Tanganyika, only a few native soldiers, known as Askaris, and a handful of officers. So all of us civilian men were made Special Reservists. I was given an armband and put in charge of twenty Askaris. My little troop and I were ordered to block the road that led south out of Tanganyika into neutral Portuguese East Africa. This was an important job, for it was along that road most of the Germans would try to escape when war was declared.

I took my happy gang with their rifles and one machine-gun and set up a road-block in a place where the road passed through dense jungle, about ten miles outside the town. We had a field telephone to headquarters which would tell us at once when war was declared. We settled down to wait. For three days we waited. And during the nights, from all around us in the jungle, came the sound of native drums beating weird hypnotic rhythms. Once, I wandered into the jungle in the dark and came across about fifty natives squatting in a circle around a fire. One man only was beating the drum. Some were dancing round the fire. The remainder were drinking something out of coconut shells. They welcomed me into their circle. They were lovely people. I could talk to them in their language. They gave me a shell filled with a thick grey intoxicating fluid made of fermented maize. It was called, if I remember rightly, Pomba. I drank it. It was horrible.

The next afternoon, the field telephone rang and a voice said, 'We are at war with Germany.' Within minutes, far away in the distance, I saw a line of cars throwing up clouds of dust, heading our way, beating it for the neutral territory of Portuguese East Africa as fast as they could go.

Ho ho, I thought. We are going to have a little battle, and I called out to my twenty Askaris to prepare themselves. But there was no battle. The Germans, who were after all only civilian townspeople, saw our machine-gun and our rifles and quickly gave themselves up. Within an hour, we had a couple of hundred of them on our hands. I felt rather sorry for them. Many I knew personally, like Willy Hink the watchmaker and Herman Schneider who owned the soda-water factory. Their only crime had been that they were German. But this was war, and in the cool of the evening, we marched them all back to Dar-es-Salaam where they were put into a huge camp surrounded by barbed wire.

The next day, I got into my old car and drove north, heading for Nairobi, in Kenya, to join the RAF. It was a rough trip and it took me four days. Bumpy jungle roads, wide rivers where the car had to be put on to a raft and pulled across by a ferryman hauling on a rope, long green snakes sliding across the road in front of the car. (NB. Never try to run over a snake because it can be thrown up into the air and may land inside your open car. It's happened many times.) I slept at night in the car. I passed below the beautiful Mount Kilimanjaro, which had a hat of snow on its head. I drove through the Masai country where the men drank cows' blood and every one of them seemed to be seven feet tall. I nearly collided with a giraffe on the Serengeti Plain. But I came safely to Nairobi at last and reported to RAF headquarters at the airport.

For six months, they trained us in small aeroplanes called Tiger Moths, and those days were also glorious. We skimmed all over Kenya in our little Tiger Moths. We saw great herds of elephants. We saw the pink flamingoes on Lake Nakuru. We saw everything there was to see in that magnificent country. And often, before we could take off, we had to chase the zebras off the flying-field. There were twenty of us training to be pilots out there in Nairobi. Seventeen of those twenty were killed during the war.

From Nairobi, they sent us up to Iraq, to a desolate airforce base near Baghdad, to finish our training. The place was called Habbaniyih, and in the afternoons it got so hot (130 degrees in the shade) that we were not allowed out of our huts. We just lay on the bunks and sweated. The unlucky ones got heat-stroke and were taken to hospital and packed in ice for several days. This either killed them or saved them. It was a fifty-fifty chance.

At Habbaniyih, they taught us to fly more powerful aeroplanes with guns in them, and we practised shooting at drogues (targets in the air pulled behind other planes) and at objects on the ground.

Finally, our training was finished, and we were sent to Egypt to fight against the Italians in the Western Desert of Libya. I joined 80 Squadron, which flew fighters, and at first we had only ancient single-seater biplanes called Gloster Gladiators. The two machine-guns on a Gladiator were mounted one on either side of the engine, and they fired their bullets, believe it or not, *through* the propeller. The guns were somehow synchronized with the propeller shaft so that in theory the bullets missed the whirling propeller blades. But as you might guess, this complicated mechanism often went wrong and the poor pilot, who was trying to shoot down the enemy, shot off his own propeller instead.

I myself was shot down in a Gladiator which crashed far out in the Libyan desert between the enemy lines. The plane burst into flames, but I managed to get out and was finally rescued and carried back to safety by our own soldiers who crawled out across the sand under cover of darkness.

That crash sent me to hospital in Alexandria for six months with a fractured skull and a lot of burns. When I came out, in April 1941, my squadron had been moved to Greece to fight the Germans who were invading from the north. I was given a Hurricane and told to fly it from Egypt to Greece and join the squadron. Now, a Hurricane fighter was not at all like the old Gladiator. It had eight Browning machine-guns, four in each wing, and all eight of them fired simultaneously when you pressed the small button on your joy-stick. It was a magnificent plane, but it had a range of only two hours' flying-time. The journey to Greece, non-stop, would take nearly five hours, always over the water. They put extra fuel tanks on the wings. They said I would make it. In the end, I did. But only just. When you are six feet six inches tall, as I am, it is no joke to be sitting crunched up in a tiny cockpit for five hours.

In Greece, the RAF had a total of about eighteen Hurricanes. The Germans had at least one thousand aeroplanes to operate with. We had a hard time. We were driven from our aerodrome outside Athens (Elevis), and flew for a while from a small secret landing-strip farther west (Menidi). The Germans soon found that one and bashed it to bits, so with the few planes we had left, we flew off to a tiny field (Argos) right down in the south of Greece, where we hid our Hurricanes under the olive trees when we weren't flying.

But this couldn't last long. Soon, we had only five Hurricanes left, and not many pilots still alive. Those five planes were flown to the island of Crete. The Germans captured Crete. Some of us escaped. I was one of the lucky ones. I finished up back in Egypt. The squadron was re-formed and re-equipped with Hurricanes. We were sent off to Haifa, which was then in Palestine (now Israel), where we fought the Germans again and the Vichy French in Lebanon and Syria.

At that point, my old head injuries caught up with me. Severe headaches compelled me to stop flying. I was invalided back to England and sailed on a troopship from Suez to Durban to Capetown to Lagos to Liverpool, chased by German submarines in the Atlantic and bombed by long-range Focke-Wulf aircraft every day for the last week of the voyage.

I had been away from home for four years. My mother, bombed out of her own house in Kent during the Battle of Britain and now living in a small thatched cottage in Buckinghamshire, was happy to see me. So were my four sisters and my brother. I was given a month's leave. Then suddenly I was told I was being sent to Washington DC in the United States of America as Assistant Air Attaché. This was January 1942, and one month earlier the Japanese had bombed the American fleet in Pearl Harbor. So the United States was now in the war as well.

I was twenty-six years old when I arrived in Washington, and I still had no thoughts of becoming a writer.

During the morning of my third day, I was sitting in my new office at the British Embassy and wondering what on earth I was meant to be doing, when there was a knock on my door. 'Come in.'

A very small man with thick steel-rimmed spectacles shuffled shyly into the room. 'Forgive me for bothering you,' he said.

'You aren't bothering me at all,' I answered. 'I'm not doing a thing.'

He stood before me looking very uncomfortable and out of place. I thought perhaps he was going to ask for a job.

'My name,' he said, 'is Forester. C. S. Forester.'

I nearly fell out of my chair. 'Are you joking?' I said.

'No,' he said, smiling. 'That's me.'

And it was. It was the great writer himself, the inventor of Captain Hornblower and the best teller of tales about the sea since Joseph Conrad. I asked him to take a seat.

'Look,' he said. 'I'm too old for the war. I live over here now. The only thing I can do to help is to write things about Britain for the American papers and magazines. We need all the help America can give us. A magazine called the *Saturday Evening Post* will publish any story I write. I have a contract with them. And I have come to you because I think you might have a good story to tell. I mean about flying.'

'No more than thousands of others,' I said. 'There are lots of pilots who have shot down many more planes than me.'

'That's not the point,' Forester said. 'You are now in America, and because you have, as they say over here, "been in combat", you are a rare bird on this side of the Atlantic. Don't forget they have only just entered the war.'

'What do you want me to do?' I asked.

'Come and have lunch with me,' he said. 'And while we're eating, you can tell me all about it. Tell me your most exciting adventure and I'll write it up for the *Saturday Evening Post*. Every little bit helps.'

I was thrilled. I had never met a famous writer before. I examined him closely as he sat in my office. What astonished me was that he looked so ordinary. There was nothing in the least unusual about him. His face, his conversation, his eyes behind the spectacles, even his clothes were all exceedingly normal. And yet here was a writer of stories who was famous the world over. His books had been read by millions of people. I expected sparks to be shooting out of his head, or at the very least, he should have been wearing a long green cloak and a floppy hat with a wide brim.

But no. And it was then I began to realize for the first time that there are two distinct sides to a writer of fiction. First, there is the side he displays to the public, that of an ordinary person like anyone else, a person who does ordinary things and speaks an ordinary language. Second, there is the secret side which comes out in him only after he has closed the door of his workroom and is completely alone. It is then that he slips into another world altogether, a world where his imagination takes over and he finds himself actually *living* in the places he is writing about at that moment. I myself, if you want to know, fall into a kind of trance and everything around me disappears. I see only the point of my pencil moving over the paper, and quite often two hours go by as though they were a couple of seconds.

'Come along,' C. S. Forester said to me. 'Let's go to lunch. You don't seem to have anything else to do.'

As I walked out of the Embassy side by side with the great man, I was churning with excitement. I had read all the Hornblowers and just about everything else he had written. I had, and still have, a great love for books about the sea. I had read all of Conrad and all of that other splendid sea-writer, Captain Marryat (*Mr Midshipman Easy*, *From Powder Monkey to Admiral*, etc.), and now here I was about to have lunch with somebody who, to my mind, was also pretty terrific.

He took me to a small expensive French restaurant somewhere near the Mayflower Hotel in Washington. He ordered a sumptuous lunch, then he produced a notebook and a pencil (ballpoint pens had not been invented in 1942) and laid them on the tablecloth. 'Now,' he said, 'tell me about the most exciting or frightening or dangerous thing that happened to you when you were flying fighter planes.'

I tried to get going. I started telling him about the time I was shot down in the Western Desert and the plane had burst into flames.

The waitress brought two plates of smoked salmon. While we tried to eat it, I was trying to talk and Forester was trying to take notes.

The main course was roast duck with vegetables and potatoes and a thick rich gravy. This was a dish that required one's full attention as well as two hands. My narrative began to flounder. Forester kept putting down the pencil and picking up the fork, and vice versa. Things weren't going well. And apart from that, I have never been much good at telling stories aloud.

'Look,' I said. 'If you like, I'll try to write down on paper what happened and send it to you. Then you can rewrite it properly yourself in your own time. Wouldn't that be easier? I could do it tonight.'

That, though I didn't know it at the time, was the moment that changed my life.

'A splendid idea,' Forester said. 'Then I can put this silly notebook away and we can enjoy our lunch. Would you really mind doing that for me?'

'I don't mind a bit,' I said. 'But you mustn't expect it to be any good. I'll just put down the facts.'

'Don't worry,' he said. 'So long as the facts are there, I can write the story. But please,' he added, 'let me have plenty of detail. That's what counts in our business, tiny little details, like you had a broken shoelace on your left shoe, or a fly settled on the rim of your glass at lunch, or the man you were talking to had a broken front tooth. Try to think back and remember everything.'

'I'll do my best,' I said.

He gave me an address where I could send the story,

and then we forgot all about it and finished our lunch at leisure. But Mr Forester was not a great talker. He certainly couldn't talk as well as he wrote, and although he was kind and gentle, no sparks ever flew out of his head and I might just as well have been talking to an intelligent stockbroker or lawyer.

That night, in the small house I lived in alone in a suburb of Washington, I sat down and wrote my story. I started at about seven o'clock and finished at midnight. I remember I had a glass of Portuguese brandy to keep me going. For the first time in my life, I became totally absorbed in what I was doing. I floated back in time and once again I was in the sizzling hot desert of Libya, with white sand underfoot, climbing up into the cockpit of the old Gladiator, strapping myself in, adjusting my helmet, starting the motor and taxiing out for take-off. It was astonishing how everything came back to me with absolute clarity. Writing it down on paper was not difficult. The story seemed to be telling itself, and the hand that held the pencil moved rapidly back and forth across each page. Just for fun, when it was finished, I gave it a title. I called it 'A Piece of Cake'.

The next day, somebody in the Embassy typed it out for me and I sent it off to Mr Forester. Then I forgot all about it.

Exactly two weeks later, I received a reply from the great man. It said:

Dear RD, You were meant to give me notes, not a finished story.
I'm bowled over. Your piece is marvellous. It is the work of a

*gifted writer. I didn't touch a word of it. I sent it at once under
your name to my agent, Harold Matson, asking him to offer it to
the Saturday Evening Post with my personal recommendation.
You will be happy to hear that the Post accepted it immediately
and have paid one thousand dollars. Mr Matson's commission is
ten per cent. I enclose his check for nine hundred dollars. It's all
yours. As you will see from Mr Matson's letter, which I also
enclose, the Post is asking if you will write more stories for them.
I do hope you will. Did you know you were a writer? With my
very best wishes and congratulations, C. S. Forester.*

'A Piece of Cake' is printed at the end of this book.*

Well! I thought. My goodness me! Nine hundred dollars! And they're going to print it! But surely it can't be as easy as all that?

Oddly enough, it was.

The next story I wrote was fiction. I made it up. Don't ask me why. And Mr Matson sold that one, too. Out there in Washington in the evenings over the next two years, I wrote eleven short stories. All were sold to American magazines, and later they were published in a little book called *Over to You*.

Early on in this period, I also had a go at a story for children. It was called 'The Gremlins', and this I believe was the first time the word had been used. In my story, Gremlins were tiny men who lived on RAF fighter-planes and bombers, and it was the Gremlins, not the enemy,

* 'A Piece of Cake' now appears in *War: Tales of Conflict and Strife*.

who were responsible for all the bullet-holes and burning engines and crashes that took place during combat. The Gremlins had wives called Fifinellas, and children called Widgets, and although the story itself was clearly the work of an inexperienced writer, it was bought by Walt Disney who decided he was going to make it into a full-length animated film. But first it was published in *Cosmopolitan Magazine* with Disney's coloured illustrations (December 1942), and from then on, news of the Gremlins spread rapidly through the whole of the RAF and the United States Air Force, and they became something of a legend.

Because of the Gremlins, I was given three weeks' leave from my duties at the Embassy in Washington and whisked out to Hollywood. There, I was put up at Disney's expense in a luxurious Beverly Hills hotel and given a huge shiny car to drive about in. Each day, I worked with the great Disney at his studios in Burbank, roughing out the story-line for the forthcoming film. I had a ball. I was still only twenty-six. I attended story-conferences in Disney's enormous office where every word spoken, every suggestion made, was taken down by a stenographer and typed out afterwards. I mooched around the rooms where the gifted and obstreperous animators worked, the men who had already created *Snow White*, *Dumbo*, *Bambi* and other marvellous films, and in those days, so long as these crazy artists did their work, Disney didn't care when they turned up at the studio or how they behaved.

When my time was up, I went back to Washington and left them to it.

My Gremlin story was published as a children's

book in New York and London, full of Disney's colour illustrations, and it was called of course *The Gremlins*. Copies are very scarce now and hard to come by. I myself have only one. The film, also, was never finished. I have a feeling that Disney was not really very comfortable with this particular fantasy. Out there in Hollywood, he was a long way away from the great war in the air that was going on in Europe. Furthermore, it was a story about the Royal Air Force and not about his own countrymen, and that, I think, added to his sense of bewilderment. So in the end, he lost interest and dropped the whole idea.

My little Gremlin book caused something else quite extraordinary to happen to me in those wartime Washington days. Eleanor Roosevelt read it to her grandchildren in the White House and was apparently much taken with it. I was invited to dinner with her and the President. I went, shaking with excitement. We had a splendid time and I was invited again. Then Mrs Roosevelt began asking me for week-ends to Hyde Park, the President's country house. Up there, believe it or not, I spent a good deal of time alone with Franklin Roosevelt during his relaxing hours. I would sit with him while he mixed the martinis before Sunday lunch, and he would say things like, 'I've just had an interesting cable from Mr Churchill.' Then he would tell me what it said, something perhaps about new plans for the bombing of Germany or the sinking of U-Boats, and I would do my best to appear calm and chatty, though actually I was trembling at the realization that the most powerful man in the world was telling me these mighty secrets. Sometimes he drove me around the estate in his car, an old Ford I think it was, that had been specially adapted for his paralysed legs. It had no pedals. All the controls were worked by his hands. His secret-service men would lift him out of his wheel-chair into the driver's seat, then he would wave them away and off we would go, driving at terrific speeds along the narrow roads.

One Sunday during lunch at Hyde Park, Franklin Roosevelt told a story that shook the assembled guests. There were about fourteen of us sitting on both sides of the long dining-room table, including Princess Martha of Norway and several members of the Cabinet. We were eating a rather insipid white fish covered with a thick grey sauce. Suddenly the President pointed a finger at me and said, 'We have an Englishman here. Let me tell you what happened to another Englishman, a representative of the King, who was in Washington in the year 1827.' He gave the man's name, but I've forgotten it. Then he went on, 'While he was over here, this fellow died, and the British for some reason insisted that his body be sent home to England for burial. Now the only way to do that in those days was to pickle it in alcohol. So the body was put into a barrel of rum. The barrel was lashed to the mast of a schooner and the ship sailed for home. After about four weeks at sea, the captain of the schooner noticed a most frightful stench coming from the barrel. And in the end, the smell became so appalling they had to cut the barrel loose and roll it overboard. But do you know *why* it stank so badly?' the President asked, beaming at the guests with that famous wide smile of his. 'I will tell you exactly why.

Some of the sailors had drilled a hole in the bottom of the barrel and had inserted a bung. Then every night they had been helping themselves to the rum. And when they had drunk it all, that's when the trouble started.' Franklin Roosevelt let out a great roar of laughter. Several females at the table turned very pale and I saw them pushing their plates of boiled white fish gently away.

All the stories I wrote in those early days were fiction, except for that first one I did with C. S. Forester. Non-fiction, which means writing about things that have actually taken place, doesn't interest me. I enjoy least of all writing about my own experiences. And that explains why this story is so lacking in detail. I could quite easily have described what it was like to be in a dog-fight with German fighters fifteen thousand feet above the Parthenon in Athens, or the thrill of chasing a Junkers 88 in and out the mountain peaks in Northern Greece, but I don't want to do it. For me, the pleasure of writing comes with inventing stories.

Apart from the Forester story, I think I have only written one other non-fiction piece in my life, and I did this only because the subject was so enthralling I couldn't resist it. The story is called 'The Mildenhall Treasure', and it's in this book.*

So there you are. That's how I became a writer. Had I not been lucky enough to meet Mr Forester, it would probably never have happened.

* 'The Mildenhall Treasure' now appears in *Deception: Tales of Intrigue and Lies*.

Now, more than thirty years later, I'm still slogging away. To me, the most important and difficult thing about writing fiction is to find the plot. Good original plots are very hard to come by. You never know when a lovely idea is going to flit suddenly into your mind, but by golly, when it does come along, you grab it with both hands and hang on to it tight. The trick is to write it down at once, otherwise you'll forget it. A good plot is like a dream. If you don't write down your dream on paper the moment you wake up, the chances are you'll forget it and it'll be gone for ever.

So when an idea for a story comes popping into my mind, I rush for a pencil, a crayon, a lipstick, anything that will write, and scribble a few words that will later remind me of the idea. Often, one word is enough. I was once driving alone on a country road and an idea came for a story about someone getting stuck in an elevator between two floors in an empty house. I had nothing to write with in the car. So I stopped and got out. The back of the car was covered with dust. With one finger I wrote in the dust the single word ELEVATOR. That was enough. As soon as I got home, I went straight to my workroom and wrote the idea down in an old red-covered school exercise-book which is simply labelled 'Short Stories'.

I have had this book ever since I started trying to write seriously. There are ninety-eight pages in the book. I've counted them. And just about every one of those pages is filled up on both sides with these so-called story ideas. Many are no good. But just about every story and every children's book I have ever written has started out as a three- or four-line note in this little, much-worn red-covered volume. For example:

> What about a chocolate factory
> That makes fantastic and marvellous
> Things — with a crazy man running it?

This became *Charlie and the Chocolate Factory*.

> A story about Mr. Fox who has a
> whole network of underground Tunnels
> leading to all the shops in the village.
> At night, he goes up through the
> floorboards and helps himself.

Fantastic Mr Fox.

> Jamaica and the small boy who saw
> a giant Turtle captured by native
> fishermen. Boy pleads with his father
> To buy Turtle and release it. Becomes
> hysterical. Father buys it. Then what?
> Perhaps boy goes with ~~or~~ joins Turtle.

'The Boy Who Talked with Animals.'

A man acquires the ability to see through playing-cards. He makes millions at casinos.

This became 'Henry Sugar'.

Sometimes, these little scribbles will stay unused in the notebook for five or even ten years. But the promising ones are always used in the end. And if they show nothing else, they do, I think, demonstrate from what slender threads a children's book or a short story must ultimately be woven. The story builds and expands while you are writing it. All the best stuff comes at the desk. But you can't even start to write that story unless you have the beginnings of a plot. Without my little notebook, I would be quite helpless.

We believe in doing good things.

That's why ten per cent of all Roald Dahl income*
goes to our charity partners. We have supported
causes including: specialist children's nurses,
grants for families in need, and educational
outreach programmes. Thank you for helping
us to sustain this vital work.

Find out more at roalddahl.com

The Roald Dahl Charitable Trust is a registered charity (no. 1119330).
*All author payments and royalty income net of third party commissions.

ROALD DAHL

Roald Dahl was a spy, ace fighter pilot, chocolate historian and medical inventor. He was also the author of *Charlie and the Chocolate Factory*, *Matilda*, *The BFG* and many more brilliant stories. He remains the World's No.1 storyteller.

CHARMING BAKER

Born in Hampshire in 1964, Charming Baker spent much of his early life travelling around the world following his father, a commando in the British Army. At the age of twelve, he and his family finally settled in Ripon, North Yorkshire. Baker left school at sixteen and worked in various manual jobs. In 1985, having gone back to college, he was accepted on to a course at the prestigious Central Saint Martins, where he later returned as a lecturer. After graduating, Baker worked for many years as a commercial artist as well as developing his personal work.

Solo exhibitions include the Truman Brewery, London, 2007, Redchurch Street Gallery, London, 2009, New York Studio Gallery, NYC, 2010, Mercer Street, London, 2011 and Milk Studios, LA, 2013. Baker has also exhibited with the Fine Art Society, collaborated with Sir Paul Smith for a sculpture entitled *Triumph in the Face of Absurdity*, which was displayed at the Victoria and Albert Museum, and continues to be committed to creating work to raise money for many charities. He has recently been commissioned to be a presenter on *The Art Show*. His work is in many international collections.

Although Baker has produced sculptural pieces in a wide and varied choice of materials, as well as many large-scale and detailed drawings, he remains primarily a painter with an interest in narrative and an understanding of the tradition of painting. Known to purposefully damage his work by drilling, cutting and even shooting it, Baker intentionally puts in to question the preciousness of art and the definition of its beauty, adding to the emotive charge of the work he produces. Indeed, Edward Lucie-Smith has described Baker's paintings as having, 'something more, a kind of romantic melancholy that is very British. And sometimes the melancholy turns out to have sharp claws. The pictures make you sit up and examine your conscience.'

Charming Baker lives and works in London.

WAR
Tales of Conflict and Strife

In war are we at our heroic best or our cowardly worst? Featuring the autobiographical stories from Roald Dahl's time as a fighter pilot in the Second World War as well as seven other tales of conflict and strife, Dahl reveals the human side of our darkest days.

Among other stories, you'll read about the pilot shot down in the Libyan desert, the fighter plane lost in mysterious thick cloud and the soldier who returns from war but has been mysteriously changed by it.

FEAR

Tales of Terror and Suspense

Do you like feeling scared? Featuring fourteen classic spine-chilling stories chosen by Roald Dahl, these terrible tales will have you shivering as you turn the pages.

They include such timeless and haunting tales as Sheridan Le Fanu's 'The Ghost of a Hand', Edith Wharton's 'Afterward', Cynthia Asquith's 'The Corner Shop' and Mary Treadgold's 'The Telephone'.

TRICKERY
Tales of Deceit and Cunning

How underhand could you be to get what you want? In these ten tales of dark and twisted trickery Roald Dahl reveals that we are at our smartest and most cunning when we set out to deceive others – and sometimes even ourselves.

Here, among others, you'll read of the husband and wife and the parting gift which rocks their marriage, the light fingered hitch-hiker and the grateful motorist, and discover how sleeping pills can aid a little bit of serious poaching.

DECEPTION
Tales of Intrigue and Lies

Why do we lie? Why do we deceive those we love most? What do we fear revealing? In these ten tales of deception Roald Dahl explores our tireless efforts to hide the truth about ourselves.

Here, among many others you'll read about how to get away with the perfect murder, the old man whose wagers end in a most disturbing payment, how revenge is sweeter when it is carried out by someone else and the card sharp so good at cheating he does something surprising with his life.

MADNESS
Tales of Fear and Unreason

Our greatest fear is of losing control – above all, of losing control of ourselves. In these ten unsettling tales of unexpected madness Roald Dahl explores what happens when we let go of our sanity.

Among other stories, you'll meet the husband with a jealous fixation on the family cat, the landlady who wants her guests to stay for ever, the man whose taste for pork leads him astray and the wife with a pathological fear of being late.